JUSTICE FOR ALL

Justice for All

An Introduction to

THE SOCIAL TEACHING OF
THE CATHOLIC CHURCH

REV. BENJAMIN L. MASSE, S.J.

THE BRUCE PUBLISHING COMPANY • MILWAUKEE

261.8
M

IMPRIMI POTEST:
> JOHN J. McGINTY, S.J.
> Provincial, New York Province
> Society of Jesus

NIHIL OBSTAT:
> JOHN F. MURPHY, S.T.D.
> Censor librorum

IMPRIMATUR:
> ✠ WILLIAM E. COUSINS
> Archbishop of Milwaukee

> May 27, 1964

Preface

The idea of this book was born one day when a priest burdened with parish cares confided that he had never finished Pope John's *Mater et Magistra* because much of the encyclical was beyond his reach.

Even if that priest is not typical of the American clergy, his reaction to *Mater et Magistra* is common enough to suggest that many Catholics, clerical as well as lay, find the social encyclicals of the Popes forbiddingly difficult reading. Whatever the cause, these documents are not being read and studied as widely as they ought to be. Although a certain amount of the Church's social teaching no doubt trickles down to the people through the press, pulpit, classroom, and lecture platform, one can scarcely say that American Catholics as a group are well instructed in this area of their Church's teaching. Even those among them who have been educated in Catholic schools are frequently unfamiliar with *Rerum Novarum, Quadragesimo Anno*, and other basic social pronouncements of the Holy See. Yet Pope John strongly insists in *Mater et Magistra* that "Christian social doctrine is an integral part of the Christian conception of life."

This book aims to help bridge the gap between papal social documents and those Catholics who think seriously, or would like to think seriously, about the great socioeconomic problems of our times. It can be considered an introduction to the Church's social teaching written against an American background. It is not, therefore, a book for scholars. In the spirit of *Mater et Magistra*, I have avoided controversies that are of more interest to theologians and social scientists than they are to the general reader. Those who are concerned about the finer shadings of the virtue of justice, or about the exact nature of the *ordines* of Pope Pius XI will have to look elsewhere. What is needed today is not another round of those "interminable discussions" mentioned in *Mater et Magistra*, but an effort to move from such agreement as exists to "efficacious and suitable action."

Since the Rev. John F. Cronin, S.S., in his *Social Principles and Economic Life* (Bruce, 1959), has already done a magisterial bibliographical job for Catholic social teaching, it is hardly necessary to repeat that work here. Furthermore, the America Press and Paulist Press editions of *Mater et Magistra* contain numerous helpful references. For those who do not have Father Cronin's book at their elbow, a brief bibliographical note will be found at the end of this text.*

The years immediately ahead of us are bound to be precarious and difficult. The world of the nineteenth century, so proud of its achievements and so confident of the future, has become a political and social shambles. If a better world arises from its ruins, this will only be because men who worship God are prepared to face the implications of their faith for the problems of the twentieth century and are courageous enough to translate them into programs of action. The world will not be won by comfortable defenders of the status quo, no matter how ringing their denunciations of communism may be. This, I take it, is the urgent message of those great documents of Pope John XXIII, *Mater et Magistra* and *Pacem in Terris*. May this small book help in some way to make them better known and loved.

I am grateful to all the publishers who have given permission to quote from their books. In writing the first two chapters, I leaned heavily on Joseph F. Flubacher's *The Concept of Ethics in the History of Economics* — a book that deserves to be better known than it is. I am also indebted to all my colleagues on the staff of *America*, especially to the Rev. Donald R. Campion, S.J., who read the entire manuscript and made numerous helpful suggestions.

BENJAMIN L. MASSE, S.J.

To save space, abbreviations of the Latin titles of the encyclicals are used in all textual references. Rerum Novarum ("On the Condition of Workers") becomes RN; Quadragesimo Anno ("On Reconstructing the Social Order") becomes QA; Divini Redemptoris ("Atheistic Communism") becomes DR; Casti Connubii ("On Christian Marriage") becomes CC; Mater et Magistra ("Christianity and Social Progress") becomes MM; Pacem in Terris ("Peace on Earth") becomes PT.

Contents

JUSTICE FOR ALL

CHAPTER 1

Religion and Economics

Two thousand years ago, the Second Person of the Blessed Trinity became man, lived on this little planet of ours for a brief thirty-three years, and then went home to His heavenly Father.

Life has never been the same since. For those who believe in Christ Jesus, it has taken on new and richer meaning. They see in the Son of Man the Redeemer promised by God after Adam's sin in the Garden of Eden. To them He is the Way that God wishes all men to follow, the Truth He wants them to believe, the Life He offers as the only answer to the longings of their hearts for happiness. Their hope that the drama of human existence, with all its doubt and suffering, somehow makes sense resides solely in Him. For Christians the cross on which the Son of God died is at once the most sacred and most joyful of symbols.

More than this Christians believe. On the testimony of the Good Tidings, the Gospels of Matthew, Mark, Luke, and John, they believe that Jesus Christ established a Church to continue His redemptive mission to the end of time. Just as He taught God's truth to the men of the first century, and gave to as many as received Him a share in divine life, so would the Church, His Mystical Body, teach and sanctify the generations to come. It was to be, in the words of Pope John XXIII, the Teacher and Mother of all nations.

Catholics have never questioned the Church's right and duty to teach all truth necessary for salvation, whether that truth was made known by divine revelation, as in the Old and New Testaments, or was discovered by human reason. In modern times, however, as public life became more and more secularized, some confusion arose over the role of religion in

1

economic and political affairs. There were demands, not all of them from non-Catholic sources, that the Church retreat to the sacristy and restrict itself to purely ecclesiastical matters. While no one went so far as to claim that the divine prohibition of stealing should be abolished, many held that the Church's application of the Seventh Commandment to economic affairs, as well as its emphasis on the virtues of justice and charity, should be rigidly limited. The whole process of producing and distributing wealth, it was said, was governed by laws of nature no less inexorable in their operation than are the physical laws. Just as it was unthinkable that the Church, in striving to save men, should attempt to interfere with the law of gravity, so it was contrary to reason that it should try to tinker with the law of supply and demand.

As a consequence of this type of reasoning, the way was opened to a disastrous ethical split between private and public life. On the private level, in their family lives and social relationships, men continued to heed the teachings of religion. On the public level, they followed the rules, and adapted themselves to the practices of the marketplace. That these rules and practices frequently conflicted with their inmost religious beliefs was deemed regrettable but was widely accepted as necessary. In a world where "business is business," there was no room for moral sentiment.

Today the climate has changed. It has been changing in fact for a long time. It is now more than forty years since the late R. H. Tawney delivered a series of lectures at King's College, London, on "Religious Thought on Social Questions in the Sixteenth and Seventeenth Centuries." (The lectures were subsequently published in book form under the title *Religion and the Rise of Capitalism*.) In his opening lecture, Tawney referred to a growing doubt about the prevailing concept of economic life:

> Has religious opinion in the past regarded questions of social organization and economic conduct as irrelevant to the life of

the spirit, or has it endeavored not only to Christianize the individual but to make a Christian civilization? Can religion admit the existence of a sharp antithesis between personal morality and the practices which are permissible in business? Does the idea of a Church involve the acceptance of any particular standard of social ethics, and, if so, ought a Church to endeavor to enforce it as among the obligations incumbent on its members? Such are a few of the questions which men are asking today. . . .
(*Religion and the Rise of Capitalism*, Pelican Books ed., p. 30.)

To appreciate how far this questioning has gone, we have only to recall that just two generations ago a great American industrialist, implying an invidious identity between the profitable and the ethical, announced that "whatever is good business is also good morals." Obviously, no business leader nowadays would dream of spouting such patently secularistic nonsense — not in public, at any rate.

The way is open, therefore, to reestablish the traditional place of morality in the marketplace. With the economic systems of the free world under relentless communist attack, the shift in attitude toward the relationship between religion and economics has come none too soon. The long effort of the Catholic Church in this field, going back to Pope Leo's socioeconomic encyclical *Rerum Novarum* in 1891 (and even further in several European countries), seems to have a better chance of success today than ever before.

I

There are good reasons, then, why a Church primarily intent on the spiritual well-being of men cannot be indifferent to the way in which they go about the absorbing business of producing and distributing wealth.

First of all, the Church as teacher must explain and apply the moral law of God. Since God's law extends to all human acts, commanding that good be done and evil be avoided, it obviously includes the economic sphere. Nor is the Church's teaching role restricted to individual conduct. In the nature of things, it must include the institutional framework within which the economic process takes place. If the framework is bad, if markets are rigged, for instance, or a pattern of graft exists, the God-fearing man is placed in an intolerable position. All too often he must violate his conscience or face bankruptcy. Similarly, a member of a lily-white trade union must sometimes close his eyes to racial injustice or risk losing his job.

In the second place, the Church as mother must be interested in the total well-being of her children. Since men are not disembodied spirits, the needs of the body necessarily have some connection with the health of the soul. Pope Pius XI refers to this in the following passage from *Quadragesimo Anno:*

> For then only will the social economy be rightly established and attain its purposes when all and each are supplied with all the goods that the wealth and resources of nature, technical achievement, and the social organization of economic life can furnish. And these goods ought indeed to be enough both to meet the demands of necessity and decent comfort and to advance people to that happier and fuller condition of life which, when it is wisely cared for, is not only no hindrance to virtue but helps it greatly (n. 75).

Furthermore, the goal of God's children is not merely heavenly bliss but also happiness here on earth. Were the Church to ignore this, it would not be faithful to the example of its Founder. Pope John recalls in *Mater et Magistra* how our Lord on one occasion cried out: "I have compassion on this multitude" (Mk 8:2). If the Church lacked this compassion, how could it be the true Bride of Christ?

II

From the foregoing it can easily be deduced that the concern of the Church with economic affairs is limited to their moral aspects. It professes no technical competence in the field. Accordingly, those who approach papal teaching — or read this book — with a view to finding a Christian economic theory are bound to be disappointed. The Catholic Church has no economic system. While insisting on the Church's jurisdiction over "all things that are connected with the moral law," Pope Pius XI carefully noted that its intervention in the economic order did not extend to technical matters, for which the Church "is neither suitably equipped nor endowed by office" (QA, n. 41). Should anyone seek to learn the purpose of economic activity in God's plan for life, or wish to know the proper attitude toward material possessions, or seek light on the rights and duties of employers and workers, the Church has an authoritative answer. If, however, one wishes an opinion on the effect of this or that fiscal policy on the economic growth rate, or wants advice on the best means of coping with a wave of inflation or a threat of deflation, the Church can be of no help. The claims of morality on economic activity do not destroy the legitimate independence of economic science.

In the following paragraphs Pope Pius XI clearly sets forth both the distinction between economics and ethics and the relationship between them:

> Even though economics and moral science employs each its own principles in its own sphere, it is an error, nevertheless, to say that the economic and moral orders are so distinct from and alien to each other that the former depends in no way on the latter. Certainly, the laws of economics, as they are termed, being based on the very nature of material things and on the capacities of the human body and mind, determine the limits of what productive human effort can and cannot attain in the economic field, and by what means. Yet it is reason itself that clearly shows, on the basis of the individual and social nature of things and of men, the purpose which God ordained for all economic life.
>
> But it is only the moral law which, just as it commands us to seek our supreme and last end in the whole scheme of our activity, so likewise commands us to seek directly in each kind of activity those purposes which we know that nature, or rather God, the Author of nature, established for that kind of action, and in orderly relationship to subordinate such immediate purposes to our supreme and last end (QA, nn. 42–43).

Most economists today would accept that reasoning. They

agree that their science cannot ignore value judgments. In the preface to his *Principles of Economics*, the great Alfred Marshall wrote that "ethical forces are among those of which the economist has to take account." He rejected as doomed to failure all attempts "to construct an abstract science with regards to the actions of an 'economic man,' who is under no ethical influences and who pursues pecuniary gain warily and energetically, but mechanically and selfishly" (p. vi).

Fairly early in his career, John Maynard Keynes, the most influential economist of his generation, began to wonder "whether the material advantages of keeping business and religion in different compartments are sufficient to balance the moral disadvantages" (*Laissez-Faire and Communism*, p. 44). It did not take him long to resolve his doubt. In *Essays in Persuasion*, he wrote:

> The transition from economic anarchy to a regime which deliberately aims at controlling and directing economic forces in the interests of social justice and social stability, will present enormous difficulties both technical and political. I suggest, nevertheless, that the true destiny of New Liberalism is to seek their solution (p. 335).

The insistence of the popes that religion and ethics ought to set the goals of economic activity, and that economic science should determine the feasibility of the means of achieving them has become respectable doctrine.

The fact that the Church has no economic theory does not mean, however, that it cannot be said to have a body of social doctrine. Although it is true that this social doctrine is merely a synthesis of moral principles — derived from revelation and the natural law — which the Church applies to economic activity, history justifies using the word "social" to describe it. The crisis in society that led Pope Leo XIII to write *Rerum Novarum* was known to the men of the nineteenth century as the "social question." It sprang from the maldistribution of income and the embittered relations between employers and workers that developed in the course of the Industrial Revolution. It was natural and logical, then, that Pope Leo's contribution to a solution of the "social question" should come to be known as the Church's social doctrine.

This is the doctrine, incidentally, which Pope John calls, in *Mater et Magistra*, "an integral part of the Christian conception of life" (n. 222), and which he insists must be taught and propagated in every possible way (cf. n. 223). It is not a teaching, therefore, that Catholics are free to accept or reject as the spirit moves them, or as their pocketbook interests dictate. Although encyclical letters, the means by which this social doctrine has been chiefly given to the world, are not solemn pronouncements *ex cathedra*, and therefore infallible (although individual statements may be infallible from other sources), they are highly authoritative documents. They must be received as coming from the supreme teaching authority in the Church.

It does not follow from this, however, that every sentence in the social encyclicals is to be accepted as authoritative teaching. Side by side with statements of moral truth occur informed opinions, historical judgments and exhortations to courses of action which, though appealing to knowledgeable men, are not strictly obligatory. To all such passages, the Popes expect respectful consideration, not unquestioning assent.

For instance, in discussing the current migration of peoples from country to city, which has created vast new urban slum areas in many underdeveloped countries, Pope John says that this is often due "to a variety of factors over and above those directly linked to economic development." That he is here only expressing an opinion is obvious from the way he couches his thought. "We think," the sentence begins (MM, n. 124).

In the same way when Pope Pius XI recommends in *Quadragesimo Anno* that the wage contract be changed to give workers a share in ownership, profits, or management, he clearly indicates that this progressive development is not a universal demand of the moral law. "We consider it more advisable," he writes, that this be done "so far as is possible" (n. 65).

In reading the encyclicals, we should pay close attention both to what the Popes say and how they say it. If we do this, we shall not confuse what is proposed for our belief with what is offered for our earnest consideration.

III

Before proceeding to a more detailed study of the Church's social doctrine, two additional generalizations may be helpful.

The first is that a true concept of man is basic to the Church's teaching on the economic order. In the Christian scheme of life, the individual man possesses an inherent dignity that proceeds from his origin and destiny. He is a creature of God redeemed by Christ and destined to be united some day with his Maker for all eternity. To treat man, therefore, as a mere object or thing, as a cog in the mechanism of society, as a means to an end, no matter how good and desirable that end may be, is to violate the work of God's hands. Hence arises the Church's opposition to any economic or political system that completely subordinates man to the good of a class, a race, or the state. Because he is a creature of God, man has certain moral powers, called rights, that spring from his nature and are, as the American Declaration of Independence proclaims, "unalienable." Their exercise is essential to the discharge of those duties which God has imposed on all men as a condition for salvation. It is only through the exercise of these rights that man develops his capacities and achieves the perfection of his personality.

On the other hand, man is a social being. He is destined to work out his perfection in and through society. He has duties to others, as well as to himself, and the discharge of these duties inevitably places restrictions on the exercise of his rights. A man certainly has the right, for instance, to be present in church for divine service, for in this way he fulfills his obligation to worship God. But he may not exercise this right if his presence in church would endanger the health of others. A man afflicted with smallpox, or some other contagious disease, has a duty to stay at home.

This brings us to the concept of the common good — defined as the well-being of society as a whole — which is also an essential element of the Church's social teaching. By a kind of paradox, man achieves his personal development, not by attempting to live as a self-sufficient, rugged individualist, but through a rational, loving service of his fellowmen. Society exists for him, for his full expansion as a human being, but he can achieve his individual goal only through devotion to society. "Individual men," according to Pope John, "are of necessity the foundation, the cause and the reason for the existence of all social institutions" (MM, n. 219). At the same time, individual men are obliged to cooperate with the social institutions they create. As Pope Pius XI taught in *Divini Redemptoris*, social justice requires "of each individual that which is necessary for the common good" (n. 71).

The Christian belief in the dignity and social nature of man runs like a golden thread through the Church's social doctrine. It binds teachings on ownership, work, organization, income distribution and government into a unified whole that offers a sound basis for mediating the claims of freedom and authority — for safeguarding both individual rights and the demands of the public good. It is hard to see how a democratic society can rest secure on any other foundation.

The second observation is that the Church's social teaching is not Catholic, or even Christian, in a restricted, sectarian sense. We are not dealing here with such doctrines as the primacy and infallibility of the successors of St. Peter, which set Catholics apart from other Christians, or with beliefs in the Trinity or the divinity of Christ, which are peculiar to Christians. Although the social encyclicals of the Popes are customarily addressed to Catholics, they are intended for a much wider audience. Pope John made this explicit in *Pacem in Terris* when, to the traditional greeting with which every encyclical begins, he added the words, "and to all men of good will." In the Church's practice, that phrase includes at the least all men who believe in God and acknowledge a duty to serve Him by obeying His law.

God has indeed promulgated His law in two ways. He has communicated it *directly* to men, as He did to Moses on Mount Sinai, or as Christ, the Messiah, did in the Sermon on the Mount. He has also given it to men *indirectly* by impressing it, as St. Paul says, on human nature itself (cf. Rom 2:15). In the first manner, man knows God's law by faith; in the second, by natural reason. (In fact, man has over the centuries come to know many of God's laws in both ways. So it is with the Ten Commandments, which God gave to Moses on tablets of stone, but which can also be known, at least in large measure, through the light of reason.)

In composing their encyclicals, the Popes have made some direct use of supernatural revelation, as we find it in Scripture and the living tradition of the Church. They have relied much more heavily, however, on reason. If this emphasis needs justification, one can find it in the ancient belief of the Church that in elevating man to a supernatural state God did not destroy the natural order but rather built on it. Just as the physical laws of the universe continue to operate as if man had not been given a supernatural destiny, so, too, do the moral laws which God stamped on the human conscience retain their validity. These laws, which are known as the divine natural law, bind all human beings.

Furthermore, since society is made up of men of many religious beliefs, the Church's social teaching would have only a limited appeal if the Popes had derived it exclusively, or even mainly, from supernatural sources. By speaking in terms of justice and right reason, they could hope for a wide response to their doctrine. For these moral concepts are familiar to men of all times and in all places.

Finally, the nature of the modern social question no doubt itself helped to determine the character of the Church's answer to it. The great struggle for men's minds between nineteenth-century capitalism and Marxian socialism was waged on a rationalist basis. Neither Adam Smith, whose *Wealth of Nations* profoundly influenced what later came to be known as the capitalistic system, nor the father of communism, Karl Marx, appealed to supernatural principles. If the Church's social doctrine was to impress modern men as germane to the controversy, it had to be written in terms with which the participants in the controversy were familiar.

This does not mean that we cannot properly speak of a *Catholic* social doctrine. The doctrine, after all, has been developed and taught by the Church in its role as divinely constituted authority on all matters of moral and religious truth, whether that truth is known by reason or revelation.

Nor does this mean that supernatural religion is irrelevant to the social question. The contrary is true. Without the powerful support that religion lends to human motivation, the theoretical framework of a just social order would remain only a beautiful ideal. This is all the more true since we are dealing with a field in which "the boundless appetite for riches" can easily silence the small still voice of conscience or grossly distort it. Unless men resolve to serve God in their capacity of economic agents, all efforts to build a just society will inevitably fail. "Truly," wrote Pope Pius XI in *Quadragesimo Anno*, "if we look into the matter more carefully and thoroughly, we shall clearly see that, preceding this ardently desired social restoration, there must be a renewal of Christian spirit . . . lest all our efforts be wasted and our house be builded not on a rock but on shifting sand" (n. 127).

CHAPTER 2

Historical Perspectives

In the days of Hosiah, king of Judah, and of Jeroboam, king
of Israel, the voice of the Prophet Amos thundered in the land.
And he said:

> Hear this, you who trample upon the needy, and bring the
> poor of the land to an end, saying "When will the new moon be
> over, that we may sell grain? And the sabbath, that we may
> offer wheat for sale, that we may make the ephah small and the
> shekel great, and deal deceitfully with false balances, that we
> may buy the poor for silver and the needy for a pair of sandals,
> and sell the refuse of the wheat?"
> The Lord has sworn by the pride of Jacob: "Surely I will
> never forget any of their deeds. . . .
> "I will turn your feasts into mourning, and all your songs
> into lamentation; I will bring sackcloth upon all loins, and bald-
> ness on every head; I will make it like the mourning for an only
> son, and the end of it like a bitter day" (8:4–10).

Over the centuries, the Church has played many variations
on the theme of Amos. It has, with St. Ambrose, condemned
the wealthy who "strive to drive off the poor man from his
little acre and turn out the needy from the boundaries of his
ancestral fields." It has reminded men, as recorded by St. Luke,
that "a man's life does not consist in the abundance of things
which he possesses." It has exclaimed with the Master: "How
hardly shall they that have riches enter into the Kingdom of
God!" Repeating the warning: "You cannot serve God and
mammon," it has never ceased preaching that it is only the
"poor in spirit" who are blessed by God.

Not that the Church has ever condemned wealth, anymore
than our Lord did, nor frowned on honest efforts to acquire it.
But it has always insisted that men must ever keep before their

eyes the one thing that alone is necessary: Their eternal salvation. Should they acquire property, they are to regard themselves not as absolute owners, free to do with it as they see fit, but rather as stewards who on Judgment Day will be solemnly required to account for their stewardship.

In medieval times, these gospel attitudes, together with the insights of Greek philosophy, were incorporated into Canon Law and the *Summae* of the theologians. As a result, the guild system that arose in Europe and paralleled the growth of towns developed within an ethical framework that stressed justice and aimed at preventing men from taking advantage of their brothers. The doctrine of the just price, the prohibition of usury (understood in the sense of taking interest on non-productive loans), the safeguards against monopoly, the rules for apprentices, and the codes of the master craftsmen — all reflected the primacy of morals in economic life. Never before nor since has an entire society tried so openly, and with so much success, to subordinate the process of producing and distributing wealth to a Christian vision of the world.

What we now know as Catholic social doctrine owes a great deal to those early efforts to understand and practice the implications of the Gospels for the bread-and-butter affairs of life. Three great developments, however, the Industrial Revolution, the rise of a free market economy (in which values are determined solely by the law of supply and demand), and the birth of economics as an independent science, all occurring toward the end of the eighteenth century, forced upon the Church a detailed and systematic reconsideration of the relationship of religion and ethics to the marketplace. The fruits of that study, which began fairly early in the nineteenth century, are what we know today as the Church's social doctrine. Its first official expression was the encyclical *Rerum Novarum* of Pope Leo XIII.

I

It is interesting to speculate on what the course of the

modern world might have been if the revolutionary shift from handicraft to machine production had taken place while religion was still the dominant public force in European life. Almost certainly economic science would have developed — as it did in fact begin — as an integral part of the discipline of ethics, and the anarchic idea that the wealth-producing activities of men can be separated from morals would never have gained currency. In that case, the tragic aberration of communism, which fed on the injustices that accompanied the Industrial Revolution, might never have happened.

Actually, by the middle of the eighteenth century, a reaction against the prevailing mercantilist system had become overdue. With the decline of the guilds and the rise of national states, the pendulum had swung too close to public authority and too far from individual liberty.

Mercantilism had arisen in the first place because sixteenth-century Europe was still near enough in spirit to the Ages of Faith to understand that economic activity, since it is of primary concern to the community, cannot be left completely free. Some agency had to assume the regulatory function which merchant and craft guilds, inspired by the teaching of the Church, had discharged during the Middle Ages. As markets widened with the spread of trade to newly discovered continents, it was clear that only national governments could cope with the problem. Kings and their ministers became the arbiters of economic activity. Such was the mercantilist system.

It was, perhaps, inevitable that in a still largely autocratic age the hand of government should press too heavily on people, and that state monopolies and a spate of regulations would curb legitimate economic freedom. In such circumstances, men started to ask: "How can the wealth of nations be increased and the material lives of people be made more rewarding?"

That was the question which occupied a group of eighteenth-century thinkers known as the Physiocrats. Revolting against mercantilism, which had become, they thought, not only excessively bureaucratic but too materialistic as well, they proposed a wider field for individual liberty. Adopting the slogans *laissez faire, laissez passer* ("keep hands off," "let things alone") they urged that individuals be allowed to pursue their economic interests with a minimum of government interference. In developing their ideas on prices, tariffs, taxes, and trade, they helped lay the foundations of modern economic science.

About the same time, a Scottish philosopher named Adam Smith was teaching similar ideas in his ethics course at the University of Edinburgh. Bringing to his task a wide and detailed knowledge of economic phenomena, he published in 1776 *An Inquiry Into the Nature and the Causes of the Wealth of Nations*. The book was to become, not entirely according to the intentions of its author, the bible of the new capitalism. It won for him the title of founder of modern economic science.

Like the Physiocrats, Smith stressed freedom of enterprise. He pleaded for an end to restrictions on the economic activities of individuals, for the destruction of monopolies, for the removal of restraints on trade, and for government abdication of all economic functions except the negative ones of policing private contracts and preventing excesses dangerous to individual freedom and the welfare of society. As far as possible he wanted conditions to be such that each individual could pursue his economic interests without undue interference from public authority. He believed that thereby the stimulus of competition would increase wealth and lead automatically to the material well-being of society.

Adam Smith had no intention of cutting economics adrift from ethics, nor had the Physiocrats. Neither were they blind to the need of some social control over man's acquisitive instincts. Purged of excesses, their systems of "natural liberty" could, perhaps, have been baptized.

That the ceremony never took place was no doubt due to a number of causes. The main one, however, was the outrageous lengths to which the successors of Adam Smith and the Physiocrats, especially in England, pushed the doctrine of individual liberty. In the hands of men like David Ricardo,

Jeremy Bentham, Herbert Spencer, and the members of the so-called Manchester School, notably Sir Robert Peel and Richard Cobden, the individual was freed from all curbs on the pursuit of self-interest. The economic system itself was declared independent of ethical rules, as well as of government controls. It was autonomous, subject only to its own laws, with which men had no more right to interfere than they had with the laws of physics or biology.

Thus was born the system of economic liberalism. Known also as economic individualism, or laissez-faire capitalism, it dominated the industrial development of the modern world until almost yesterday.

There can be no question that the combination of a free market with mechanized, factory production vastly increased the wealth of nations. There can be no question also that it did so at enormous social cost considered by many as prohibitive. As the nineteenth century wore on, the misery of the working masses and the protests of reformers led governments, contrary to the principles of economic liberalism, to intervene in the market. Their efforts at regulation were, alas, too modest and too late. In 1848 the *Communist Manifesto* summoned the workers of the world to unite. They had nothing to lose, said the youthful Karl Marx and Friedrich Engels, but their chains. And so the die was cast for revolution, the bitter fruits of which the divided world of the twentieth century is still sadly harvesting.

Such was the background against which Leo XIII wrote *Rerum Novarum*.

II

The objective of *Rerum Novarum* was to save society from chaos by putting an end to the revolutionary struggle between economic liberalism and Marxist socialism. Pope Leo's point of departure was God's plan for economic life. With this as a measure, he examined both laissez-faire capitalism and the

Marxist reaction to it, and found them both gravely wanting. Then he went on to state the moral principles, applicable to property, wages, industrial relations, private organizations and government, that must undergird a just social order.

Basically, what Leo XIII condemned in economic liberalism was its amorality. If the play of competitive forces operating in a completely free market is the sole and exclusive regulating principle of economic life, no additional rules, ethical or otherwise, are either necessary or possible. To say that interest rates are usurious, or that prices are outrageously high and wages oppressively low, or that the workday is inhumanly long is beside the point. All these elements of the market process are determined by an impersonal, mechanical law that allows no room for those individual decisions with which ethics and religion are concerned. In such a system, the only role left to conscience and religion is the ameliorative one of binding up the wounds incurred in the pitiless, impersonal, competitive struggle. Since there is no place for justice, there remains nothing except charity to keep society from becoming a naked jungle.

Unless the Church was prepared, then, to accept a state of affairs in which might makes right and only the fittest survive, it had to condemn laissez-faire capitalism. This Pope Leo did. He said that it was an inhuman system, and that its fruits were bound to be what they actually were — the exploitation and degradation of an entire class of society. Under it, he charged, surveying the system toward the end of the nineteenth century, workers had been handed over, "each alone and defenseless, to the inhumanity of employers and the unbridled greed of competitors" (RN, n. 6).

It must be carefully noted that Pope Leo did not reject all competition as evil, any more than he condemned individual initiative and the profit motive as such. What he excoriated was the exaggeration of these good things by economic liberalism, since this had the effect of freeing men in their capacity of economic agents from all moral and social restraints. The result could only be disruptive of the social order. As Pope Pius XI wrote forty years later:

> Just as the unity of human society cannot be founded on opposition of classes, so also the right ordering of economic life cannot be left to a free competition of forces. For from this source, as from a poisoned spring, have originated and spread all the errors of individualist economic teaching. Destroying through forgetfulness or ignorance the social and moral character of economic life, it held that economic life must be considered and treated as altogether free from, and independent of, public authority, because in the market, that is, in the free struggle of competitors, it would have a principle of self-direction which governs it much more perfectly than would the intervention of any created intellect. But free competition, while justified and certainly useful provided it is kept within certain limits, clearly cannot direct economic life — a truth which the outcome of the application in practice of the tenets of this evil individualistic spirit has more than sufficiently demonstrated (QA, n. 88).

In the chapter to follow, we shall deal with economic liberalism in greater detail. Meanwhile, even though some repetition is involved, Pope John's admirably clear and pithy synopsis of the Leonine case against economic liberalism deserves to be quoted here. The following paragraphs are from *Mater et Magistra:*

> As is well known, the prevalent view of the economic world at that time, one that exerted a fairly great influence in practice, was an entirely naturalistic one. It denied any connection between the laws of economics and those of morality. According to it, the only motive of economic action was personal profit. The supreme rule regulating relations between economic agents was to be found in uncontrolled free competition. Prices of goods and services, interest on capital, profits and wages were determined, in a more or less mechanical fashion, solely by the laws of the market place. Government, it was held, should be carefully restrained from any intervention in the economic field. At the same time, trade unions, according to circumstances in different countries, were either entirely forbidden, tolerated or recognized as having legal standing only in private law.
> In the economic world of the day, as a result, the law of the

strongest came to be fully justified on theoretical grounds, and in practice it likewise governed business relations between men. The upshot was a profound dislocation of the entire economic order (nn. 11–12).

The main reason for Pope Leo's rejection of Marxist socialism was not the vigor of its protest against capitalistic excesses but the immorality and impracticality of its program of reform.

Karl Marx postulated an irreconcilable conflict between those who owned the means of production (the bourgeois capitalists) and their hired workers (the propertyless proletariat). His solution to the conflict was to intensify it by every possible means, with the ultimate aim of establishing a dictatorship of the proletariat. The new order would be based on public ownership of the means of production, transport, and exchange. All inequalities would be abolished: "From each according to his ability; to each according to his needs."

To Pope Leo, the communist remedy, with its stress on class warfare, was worse than the capitalist disease. Not only were all men brothers, since they had God for a common Father, but the employer-worker relationship itself, while not without elements of conflict, reflected a basic community of interest — the joint production, for the mutual benefit of the producers, of a good or service for society. Furthermore, the destruction of private ownership would violate the natural rights of individuals and would, therefore, be unjust. Finally, the goal of a classless society, in which all inequalities would be done away with, was an impossible and utterly unrealistic objective. As Pope Leo wrote:

> Apart from the injustice involved, it is also only too evident what turmoil and disorder would obtain among all classes, and what a harsh and odious enslavement of citizens would result. . . . If incentives to ingenuity and skill in individual persons were to be abolished, the very fountains of wealth would necessarily dry up; and the equality conjured up by the Socialist imagination would, in reality, be nothing but uniform wretchedness and meanness for one and all, without distinction (RN, n. 22).

The reason is that inequalities are, so to speak, built into human nature and civil society, so that those who try to eliminate them are fighting against the facts of life. To quote Pope Leo again:

Therefore, let it be laid down in the first place that a condition of human existence must be borne with, namely, that in civil society the lowest cannot be made equal with the highest. . . . There are truly very great and very many natural differences among men. Neither the talents, nor the skill, nor the health, nor the capacities of all are the same, and unequal fortune follows of itself upon necessary inequality in respect to these endowments (n. 26).

Pope Leo's condemnation of what he called the "absurd equality" of Marxist socialism did not mean approval, of course, of existing patterns of inequality. On the contrary, as we saw above, *Rerum Novarum* is a scathing indictment of the gross inequalities in nineteenth-century society that resulted from the excesses of unrestricted individualism. It was Pope Leo's stinging answer to those misguided Catholics who claimed that the Church had no right to deal with the social question and "should confine herself to preaching resignation to the poor and to exhorting the rich to generosity" (MM, n. 16).

Pope Leo's response to the pleas of the downtrodden masses of industrial workers for a better deal in life was not to eliminate inequality (since this is impossible), but to reduce it. It was to narrow the unfair, trouble-breeding gap between "extreme wealth and extreme penury" (RN, n. 66) by the practice of justice and charity. What he demanded was a kind of *proportional* equality — an equality that does not require that all differences of wealth and income among the various classes of society be removed, but only that they be kept within reasonable bounds. Although it is scarcely possible to define with mathematical precision what this means in practice, it certainly demands, at a minimum, that the poorer classes should have at their disposal all the resources needed for an appropriately human standard of living. It also means, at least implicitly, that limits of some kind must be placed on the amount of wealth that the rich classes are allowed to amass and transmit to their descendants.

This much equality, as we can see from experience, is necessary for civic harmony and peace. According to Pope Leo it is also an ethical imperative — a mandate of justice. Without it, God's plan for creation, in which natural resources are intended for the support of the whole human race, cannot be realized. Hence, as we shall see, Pope Leo and his successors insisted on widespread distribution of ownership, on just wages, and on the duty of government to have a special care for the weak, the needy, and the handicapped among its citizens.

Pope John's *Mater et Magistra* has been described as "an essay on inequality." The same might be said of all the social documents of the Popes.

III

Since the time of Leo, sweeping changes have occurred in both capitalist society and the socialist movement. These changes have naturally been reflected in the development of the Church's social doctrine.

Pope Pius XI noted in 1931 that a great concentration of wealth and power had taken place in capitalistic economies. This he attributed to the unrestricted struggle among competitors that permitted only the strongest to survive. "Free competition," he wrote in *Quadragesimo Anno*, "has destroyed itself; economic dictatorship has supplanted the free market" (n. 109). The Pope also called attention to the growing separation between ownership and management. Immense power had been concentrated in the hands of a few, "who often are not owners but only the trustees and managing directors of invested funds" (n. 105).

In a widely discussed book, *The Modern Corporation and Private Property*, which appeared two years after *Quadragesimo Anno*, A. A. Berle and Gardiner C. Means documented both papal charges. They showed (1) that control of corporate wealth

in the United States had become narrowly concentrated, and
(2) that in most cases those who occupied the seats of corporate
power were not controlling stockholders but professional managers answerable, more often than not, to themselves alone.

As a result of this vast growth in corporate market power,
economists took a fresh look at the dogmas of economic liberalism. Soon new and formidable words started appearing in books
and learned journals. There was much discussion of oligopoly
(domination of a market by a few huge sellers) and oligopsony
(domination of a market by a few big buyers). Economists
agreed that competition among corporate giants was significantly different from the models of competition constructed
by economic liberals in the nineteenth century. Prices were
no longer determined by the interaction of many buyers and
sellers, none of whom was strong enough to dominate the
market. They were "administered," that is to say, fixed by the
largest firms. In some markets, the price was set by the biggest
firm, and the other firms "followed the leader." There remained
a good deal of competition, but the emphasis now was on
quality and service, rather than on price. In fact, for many
years the U. S. Government has been trying to compel price
competition by law. Its efforts have been only partially
successful.

Just as Leo XIII denied that the economic order could be
directed by free competition alone, so Pius XI rejected economic dictatorship as a morally acceptable ruling principle.
"Free competition, kept within definite and due limits, and,
still more, economic dictatorship, must be effectively brought
under public authority in those matters which pertain to its
function" (QA, n. 110).

The economic history of the past half century records many
government attempts to oblige huge concentrations of corporate
power to serve the common good, as well as the interests of
their managers and stockholders. As Pope John observes in
Mater et Magistra, this struggle still goes on (cf. n. 104). So
does the effort to define and enforce fair competition in the

nation's markets, as even a casual study of almost any recent session of the U. S. Congress will show.

The changes that have occurred in Marxist socialism are scarcely less striking than the evolution of the capitalist system. The radical wing of the movement, fanatically intent on revolutionary class warfare and public ownership of the means of production, seized power in Russia in 1918. During the following year, it established the Third (Communist) International. The other wing, the Second (Socialist) International, committed itself to a reformist, evolutionary approach to social change. Pope Pius XI described the movement in these words:

> It not only professes the rejection of violence, but modifies and tempers to some degree, if it does not reject entirely, the class struggle and the abolition of private ownership. One might say that, terrified by its own principles and by the conclusions drawn therefrom by communism, socialism inclines toward, and in a certain measure approaches, the truths which Christian tradition has always held sacred; for it cannot be denied that its demands at times come very near those that Christian reformers of society justly insist on (QA, n. 113).

Because of these changes, some European Catholics suggested that since socialism had jettisoned so much of its Marxist cargo, Christians could in good conscience accept it. Pope Pius XI firmly disagreed. Although he welcomed these developments in socialism, the Pope could find no change in its essentially materialist philosophy of man and society. Therefore, "Religious socialism, Christian socialism," he said, "are contradictory terms; no one can be at the same time a good Catholic and a true Socialist" (QA, n. 120).

Since Pope John adopted a dominantly affirmative approach to the social problem in *Mater et Magistra*, concentrating on developing and applying the Church's own social teaching, he had little, if anything, to say about either economic liberalism or socialism. But socialism has continued to evolve. More and more the socialist parties of Western Europe, which are almost without exception staunchly anticommunist, are coming to resemble the non-Marxist socialism of the British Labor party, which the Church has never condemned. Most of them retain, however, a certain anticlerical bias as part of their inheritance from the nineteenth century. This has not prevented them from entering into government coalitions with Christian Democratic parties — which are inspired by the Church's social doctrine — in Belgium, Italy, Austria, and other European countries. The cement that holds these coalitions together is a common interest in defending social reform and democratic liberties against communist reactionaries on the left and ultraconservatives (who in economic affairs remain attached to economic liberalism) on the right.

This is the new framework within which the struggle for social justice is being carried on today. With the spread of democracy and the rise of the welfare state, the terms of the old confrontation between laissez-faire capitalism and Marxian socialism have become more or less irrelevant. Perhaps that is why Pope John emphasized the positive side of the teachings of Leo and Pius. He wanted to speak to the world of the mid-twentieth century about problems that are really bothering men and in language they could understand.

CHAPTER 3

Property Rights

The question of property, in the sense of ownership of the means of production, is central to the social problem. Even if Karl Marx had never lived or written a book, this would be true. For in the nature of things, the question of property is directly related to the key problem of socioeconomic policy, namely, how can the material resources of the world best be developed and used for the support of the whole human family.

It is clear, in the first place, that no matter how the resources of the earth are owned, whether publicly or privately, they must serve the needs of all. As Pope Leo observed, "no living being is sustained except by what the fields bring forth" (RN, n. 14). Furthermore, as people today, worried over the sharp increase of population over the past century and the prospect of even faster growth, keenly appreciate, not every system of developing the earth's resources is adequate or satisfactory. The earth must be intensely and efficiently exploited if men are to avoid hunger and deprivation and have at their disposal an ample supply of life's necessities — food, clothing, and shelter. Finally, since men are more than animals, since they have been endowed by God with intelligence and freedom and given a supernatural destiny, the process of producing and distributing wealth must be in accord with their dignity and satisfy more than merely material wants.

I

The Catholic Church teaches that a system of private ownership offers the best prospect of realizing God's purpose for natural resources.

Pope Leo cited Scripture in support of the Church's position: "Thou shalt not covet thy neighbor's wife, nor his house, nor his field, nor his maid-servant, nor his ox, nor his ass, nor anything that is his" (Dt 5:21). Were there no right to private property, most of this divine commandment would be meaningless. Furthermore, many of our Lord's parables assume the institution of private property. If private ownership was in conflict with His Father's designs for natural resources, why did He not use these opportunities to condemn it? All we find in the New Testament are warnings against the danger of wealth to salvation and the evils of exploitation, along with insistence on the duty of charity. In fact, the whole economic question is treated as a secondary matter. "Seek first the Kingdom of God" is the burden of our Lord's message.

The early Christians in Jerusalem did practice, it is true, some kind of primitive communism. "Those who owned land or houses would sell them and bring the price of what they sold and lay it at the feet of the apostles, who distributed to each according to his need" (Acts 4:34–35).

There is no record, however, that this experiment was repeated anywhere else; and although the Jerusalem community no doubt believed that what they did was pleasing to their divine Master, there is no evidence that they were acting under any command of His. It is pertinent, also, to remark that St. Peter condemned Ananias and Saphira, not for keeping part of the price for their land, but for their "lie to the Holy Spirit." They pretended that the price they laid at the feet of the Apostles was the full price (cf. Acts 5:1–10).

Except for the single reference to Deuteronomy, Pope Leo did not develop the case for private property in scriptural terms. Instead he relied on reason, perhaps because he judged that no other type of argument would meet the socialists head on, or appeal to a religiously divided world. His aim in *Rerum Novarum* is to show that nature itself demands the institution of private property.

This rational defense of private ownership is very old in Western civilization. It goes back at least to Aristotle and was elaborated by Albert the Great, Thomas Aquinas, and other medieval theologians.

In addition to contending, against Plato, that private property is essential to the institution of the family, Aristotle argued that private ownership is more conducive than common, or public, ownership to civic order and economic well-being (cf. *Politics*, II). Commenting on these points in his *Summa Theologiae*, St. Thomas observes that "disputes arise not uncommonly among those who have any possession of joint stock." He concluded, therefore, that "a peaceful state is better insured (under private property), every one being content with his lot." As for economic development and progress, Aquinas believed that without the hope of personal advantage associated with ownership men would lack the incentive to work industriously. "Every one," he wrote, "is more careful to look after what is his own private concern than after what is common to all or many, since every one avoids labor and leaves to another to do the duty that belongs to a number of persons in common . . ." (II-IIae, q. 66, a. 2).

In refuting the socialists, Pope Leo uses all these arguments, and several others besides. He elaborates the case for ownership based on the idea that a man's labor gives title to material things:

> Since man expends his mental energy and his bodily strength on procuring the goods of nature, by this very act he appropriates that part of physical nature to himself which he has cultivated. On it he leaves impressed, as it were, a kind of image of his person, so that it must be altogether just that he should possess that part as his very own and that no one in any way should be permitted to violate his right (n. 15).

A second argument, somewhat less abstract and perhaps more likely to appeal to modern minds, is based on the difference between men and animals. Unlike the brute creation, man can look ahead and plan for the future. To do this intelligently, the Pope observes, requires some stability of possession (cf. nn. 11–12).

Finally, like Aristotle, Pope Leo argues that the right of ownership is natural to man not merely as an individual but as head of a family:

> It is a most sacred law of nature that the father of a family see that his offspring are provided with all the necessities of life, and nature even prompts him to desire to provide and to furnish his children (who, in fact, reflect and in a sense continue his person) with the means of decently protecting themselves against harsh fortune in the uncertainties of life. He can do this surely in no other way than by owning fruitful goods to transmit by inheritance to his children (nn. 19–20).

From all of this Pope Leo concludes, appealing to the witness of experience and history, that

> rightly, therefore, the human race as a whole, moved in no wise by the dissenting opinions of a few, and observing nature carefully, has found in the law of nature itself the basis of the distribution of goods and, by the practice of all ages, has consecrated private possessions as something best adapted to man's nature and to peaceful and tranquil living together (n. 17).

All the successors of Leo who have dealt with the social question have felt obliged to renew his defense of private property. In doing so, Pope Pius XII and Pope John XXIII emphasized, in addition to the traditional arguments, the connection between ownership and personal liberty. They were probably led to do this by the communist seizure of power in Russia and the subsequent development of the Soviet state. What stands out in the U.S.S.R., where the means of production are state-owned, is not any lack of civic order (if order can be equated with a prisonlike regimentation) or the absence of industrial progress, but the widespread denial of personal liberty.

In an address over the Vatican Radio on September 1, 1944, the fifth anniversary of the outbreak of World War II, Pope Pius sounded the note of freedom. He said:

> Private property is in a special manner the natural fruit of labor, the product of an intense activity on the part of the man

who acquires it through his energetic will to ensure and improve, by his own forces, his own living conditions and those of his family, to create for himself and those dear to him *a field in which they may rightfully enjoy not only economic freedom but political, cultural and religious freedom as well.* (Italics added.)

Accordingly, the Pope had little sympathy with the nationalization movement that arose in Europe toward the end of World War II. In a letter to the Semaines Sociales of France, meeting at Strasbourg in July, 1946, he warned that transferring ownership of large enterprises from private to public hands might increase the mechanical, depersonalizing character of industrial work, and thus hinder rather than promote the well-being of the community. In the 1944 address already cited, Pope Pius had expressed a concern for the preservation of "small holdings in agriculture, in the arts and trades, in commerce and industry." He rejected the idea that technological progress doomed small business and foreshadowed a world dominated by giant enterprises. Through government aid and resort to the principles of cooperation, he hoped that small- and medium-size business firms and farms might come to enjoy some of the advantages of bigness and thus be able to compete successfully for customers. (In *Mater et Magistra* [nn. 84–90] Pope John repeats and develops this recommendation.) Pope Pius' motive in all this was to preserve and expand individual ownership.

By the time Pope John wrote, nationalization had ceased to be a live issue. The socialists and Christian democrats who campaigned for public ownership after the war had become disillusioned with its social fruits and had turned their attention to other means of assuring that big business serve the general welfare. In the following passage from *Mater et Magistra*, the Pope refers to the change in socialist thinking about public ownership:

Until recently some movements which have for their purpose the reconciliation of justice and liberty in society were clearly opposed to private ownership of productive goods; but now, being more fully enlightened concerning actual social conditions, they have modified their stand and are taking an essentially positive attitude toward that right (n. 110).

The occasion of Pope John's defense of private property as a guarantee of liberty was a growing doubt about the importance of the Church's traditional teaching on ownership. For several reasons, it appeared to some Catholic thinkers that under contemporary conditions the Church ought to switch its emphasis from the right to private property to other factors involved in social justice. These were said to be more practical and necessary for modern men.

It was pointed out, in the first place, that the separation of ownership from management, which Pius XI had deplored in 1931, had become more pronounced than ever. Certainly, it is obvious today that an overwhelming majority of stockholders in large corporations have no opportunity — or even desire — to exercise the initiative and responsibility associated with private property.

Furthermore, most people, either by choice or by necessity, no longer rely on ownership as the chief means of defense against the uncertainties of life. Their security against sickness, unemployment, and old age is linked to various forms of private and public insurance. The answer of the twentieth century to man's age-old quest for security is not widespread ownership but the welfare state.

Finally, men today concentrate on acquiring skills rather than property, since they have more confidence, as Pope John himself explained, "in income derived from work or rights founded on work than on income derived from capital or rights founded on capital" (n. 106). In fact, there is a growing tendency in the United States to regard rights associated with jobs — seniority rights, paid vacations, pensions, supplementary unemployment benefits, health insurance — as a form of property rights.

Except for the separation of ownership from managerial responsibility, which poses, he said, special problems for governments, Pope John accepted these developments as legitimate and even desirable. The reliance of men on work rather than on capital for their material well-being, he writes, "may no doubt be considered a step forward in the process of human civilization" (n. 107).

Nevertheless, the Pope continues, none of this justifies doubts about the continued importance of private property. Besides the fundamental consideration that private ownership is a natural right, and therefore "has a permanent validity," it is obvious that without it no system of private enterprise can exist. Yet the Pope had said earlier that the economy should be primarily "the creation of the personal initiative of private citizens" (n. 51). Where it is not, where governments deny private ownership, history and experience testify that "the fundamental manifestations of freedom are suppressed or stifled. Hence, one may justifiably conclude that the exercise of freedom finds both a guarantee and an incentive in the right of ownership" (n. 109).

II

Coupled with the papal defense of private property are urgent demands that ownership be widely distributed. Toward that end the Popes have not only insisted on just wages, which permit workers to save and invest in productive property, but have also strongly commended programs that encourage and assist employees to acquire stock in their companies. In echoing the pleas of his predecessors for worker participation in ownership, Pope John says that the current widespread business practice of financing expansion from funds generated internally — retained profits, depreciation allowances and other tax concessions — makes sharing in ownership more necessary than ever (cf. n. 75). Unless this is done, internal financing can only lead to an ever greater concentration of wealth in the hands of a minority. This is so even though investments in common stocks by insurance companies and pension funds, in which many workers have a beneficial interest, have brought about, in an indirect way, a wider distribution of ownership.

Plainly, the Popes are dissatisfied on moral grounds with the present pattern of the distribution of wealth. "The distribution of created goods . . . is laboring today," Pope Pius XI remarked, "under the gravest evils due to the huge disparity between the few exceedingly rich and the unnumbered propertyless" (QA, n. 58). Twenty years and a World War later, his successor in the See of Peter was still playing variations on the same dominant theme. The Church insists, Pope Pius XII said in a message to Spanish employers and workers on March 11, 1951, "on the need for a more just distribution of property and deplores the unnatural social situation in which an enormous mass of impoverished people live beside a small group of very rich and privileged people." And the Pope added: "You know very well that a just wage and a better distribution of natural wealth constitute two of the most impelling demands in the social program of the Church." In *Mater et Magistra*, Pope John is solicitous lest the mistakes of the nineteenth century be repeated in the twentieth. Insisting that "today more than ever the wider distribution of private property ought to be forcefully championed," he offers some advice to developing countries:

> As we have noted, the economies of an increasing number of nations are in the process of rapid development. Making wise use of proven techniques, these communities will not find it difficult to adjust their socioeconomic order in such a way as to facilitate the widest possible spread of private ownership in goods of this sort: durable consumer goods, housing, farms, one's own equipment in artisan enterprises and family-type farms, shares in middle-sized and large corporations (n. 115).

It is unfortunately true that, although the masses of workers in industrially advanced countries have made striking gains in living standards over the past several decades, ownership of productive property continues to be highly concentrated. This is true even in the United States, the most advanced of all the capitalist countries. In a study published in 1962, *The*

Share of Top Wealth-Holders in National Wealth, 1922–1956,
Robert J. Lampman, a Wisconsin University economist on
the staff of the President's Council of Economic Advisers,
found that in 1957 the richest 0.5 percent of Americans held
25 percent of the nation's wealth. Under the heading of
wealth, Professor Lampman included not only stocks, bonds,
real estate, mortgages, and insurance, but such miscellaneous
property as automobiles, livestock, pensions, and royalties. He
found that ownership of the nation's corporations was even
more narrowly concentrated. In 1953, the wealthiest 1 percent
of American adults owned 76 percent of all our corporate
stock. A more recent study, *Characteristics of Stock Ownership,* published in 1963 as part of a Ford Foundation report,
found that stock ownership continues to be narrowly concentrated. According to the authors, Jean Crockett and Irwin
Friend of the University of Pennsylvania, individuals with
annual incomes over $100,000 — less than 0.1 percent of the
population — own 19.5 percent of all corporate stock. Those
with incomes of more than $25,000 own 48 percent of the
stock. (In 1960, families and unattached individuals with annual incomes of $25,000 or more were about 1.5 percent of
all families and individuals.) The well-publicized fact that 17
million Americans owned shares of stock in 1963 — which is
the basis for the slogan, "People's Capitalism" — must be
interpreted against this background of concentrated ownership. Pope John's recommendation that workers should be
encouraged and aided to become capitalists is obviously not
without pertinence to the United States.

III

In our discussion of private property, we have deferred up
until now a consideration of its exact nature. This is a criti-
cally important question because a nation's social policy is
significantly determined by the concept of property enshrined
in its laws. Many of the great debates in the United States
over social reform, especially during the New Deal period in

the 1930's, arose from conflicting ideas on the nature of property rights. As this book is being written, Congress has split into warring factions over a proposal of the Kennedy Administration, supported too by President Johnson, to outlaw racial discrimination in business establishments serving the general public. The basis of the dispute is property rights. The same is true of current controversies over legislation banning racial discrimination in the sale and rental of houses and apartments.

When Pope Leo wrote *Rerum Novarum*, the prevailing concept of private property was the one associated with economic liberalism. Economic liberals maintained that the right of private ownership was purely individualistic and more or less absolute. By this they meant (1) that in the use of their property owners had no other obligation beyond consulting their enlightened self-interest, and (2) that so long as they acted within the law they should be free of all interference by government.

Although Pope Leo made it sufficiently clear that the right of private property which he defended against socialist attack was not the right as understood by economic liberals, so many doubts and questions arose after the appearance of *Rerum Novarum* that both Pope Pius XI and Pope Pius XII felt obliged to clarify the issue.

In his radio address on September 1, 1944, Pope Pius XII, after reiterating that the Christian conscience could not accept a social order in which private ownership was denied, went on to emphasize that it was equally opposed to an order founded on a false idea of private property. Accordingly, said the Pope,

> where, for instance, "capitalism" is based on such false concepts and arrogates to itself an unlimited right over property, without any subordination to the common good, the Church has condemned it as contrary to the natural law.

The reference here is to the concept of private property that existed under economic liberalism. The Pope makes this clear when he continues:

In defending, therefore, the principle of private property, the Church pursues a high ethico-social purpose. She does not intend to defend absolutely and simply the present state of affairs, as if she saw in it the expression of God's will, nor to defend as a matter of principle the rich and the plutocrat against the poor and the proletarian.

Far from it! . . . The Church aims rather at securing that the institution of private property be such as it should be according to the designs of God's wisdom and the dispositions of nature. . . .

What then is the right of private property "according to the designs of God's wisdom and the dispositions of nature"?

In *Quadragesimo Anno*, Pope Pius XI took up this question in great detail.

All private property, he said, has both an individual and a social aspect. It is possessed by individuals for their own legitimate purposes, such as the support of their families. At the same time, it must also serve a social purpose, since otherwise private property would defeat God's purpose for all natural resources, which is, as we have seen, the support of the entire human race. In other words, the right of private property carries with it duties to use one's possessions for social as well as personal goals. It is not an absolute right, therefore, but a right conditioned by the needs of others and the demands of the common good (cf. nn. 44–48). Consequently, the state, as guardian of the common good, has an important role in a private-property regime. In the words of Pius XI:

> To define these duties of ownership in detail when necessity requires and the natural law has not done so, is the function of those in charge of the state. Therefore, public authority, under the guiding light always of the divine natural law, can determine more accurately, upon consideration of the true requirements of the common good, what is and is not permitted to owners in the use of their property (n. 49).

Nor is government to be considered an enemy of private ownership when it discharges its supervisory and regulatory function:

When the state brings private ownership into harmony with the needs of the common good, it does not commit a hostile act against private owners but rather does them a friendly service; for it thereby effectively prevents the private possession of goods, which the Author of nature in His most wise providence ordained for the support of human life, from causing intolerable evils and thus rushing to its own destruction; it does not destroy private possessions, but safeguards them and it does not weaken private property rights, but strengthens them (n. 49).

In approaching private property, then, two extremes must be avoided. First, the individualistic aspect of ownership should not be exaggerated, for that way lies the danger of economic liberalism. Second, the social aspect must be kept in proper perspective, otherwise the road is open to collectivism (cf. QA, n. 46).

In practice, there will never be complete agreement on the government's exercise of its supervisory role. At any given time, some will always be ready to argue that the regulation of ownership should be stricter and taxes higher, whereas those who possess or manage property are almost invariably persuaded that they are being crushed by taxes and strangled with red tape. Because of unusual demands on governments today, arising from the Cold War and the desperate needs of underdeveloped countries, the tax burden in almost all the advanced nations is admittedly very heavy. It cannot be considered "crushing," however, in the sense condemned by Pope Leo and Pope Pius XI (cf. RN, n. 67; QA, n. 49). From a moral standpoint, any judgment on contemporary tax systems must begin with the proposition stated by Pope John in *Mater et Magistra*: "The fundamental principle in a system of taxation based on justice and equity is that the burdens imposed should be proportionate to the capacity of people to contribute" (n. 132). The capacity to pay of the American people as a whole, and of rich individuals and corporations in particular, is, fortunately, very large.

It might be added, also, that a just tax system will encourage the wealthy to regard ownership as stewardship. This can be done by granting exemptions for individual and corporate gifts to charitable, religious, educational, and cultural causes, as well as by special incentives to worthwhile capital expenditures. Pope Pius XI reminds us that "a person's superfluous income, that is, income which he does not need to sustain life fittingly and with dignity, is not left wholly to his own free determination. Rather, the Sacred Scriptures and the Fathers of the Church constantly declare, in the most explicit language, that the rich are bound by a very grave precept to practice almsgiving, beneficence and munificence" (QA, n. 50). And Pope John recalls in *Mater et Magistra* that "Christ Jesus frequently extends to the rich an insistent invitation to convert their material goods into spiritual wealth by conferring them on the needy" (cf. Mt 25:4–7). For in heaven "neither rust nor moth consumes, nor thieves break in and steal" (Mt 6:19–20).

The Church's defense of socially responsible private property does not exclude limited public ownership (nor, of course, the power of expropriation, provided the owners are justly recompensed). On the contrary, the moral law itself requires that some types of property be owned by the state.

"It is rightly contended," Pope Pius XI taught, "that certain kinds of property ought to be reserved to the state since they carry with them a dominating power so great that it cannot without danger to the general welfare be entrusted to private individuals" (QA, n. 114). And in *Mater et Magistra*, Pope John recognizes that the expansion of public ownership in our day is a response to special needs. (This is notably true in many underdeveloped countries, which are handicapped by shortages of private capital, as well as by shortages of everything else.) The Pope observes, however, that "the state and other agencies of public law should not extend their ownership except where evident and real needs of the common good dictate it" (n. 117).

So long as this rule is observed, it is a confusing and reprehensible misuse of words to describe all public ownership as "socialistic." For so long as this rule is observed, private property remains free to play the rich, dynamic role in society that God clearly assigned to it.

For the average American, the greatest test posed at the moment by the Church's insistence on the social aspect of private ownership is the Negro revolt against discrimination in housing.

Those who resist integration are partly influenced by economic reasons. They are apprehensive lest the entry of Negro families into their neighborhoods lower the value of their property. Unscrupulous real-estate operators frequently exploit this fear. By arranging the sale of a house in an all-white neighborhood to a Negro family, or sometimes merely by sowing rumors of such a sale, they induce a panicky feeling among the residents. All too often they are able to persuade owners to sell their homes for a fraction of their true value. This vicious tactic is called "block-busting."

Many people also oppose integration because they fear a lowering of the cultural and moral tone of their neighborhoods. When associated, as it often is, with a concern for the well-being of children, this fear generates very strong and highly dangerous emotions.

In some localities, joint committees of whites and Negroes have striven with considerable success to promote better understanding between the races and thus smooth the path to peaceful integration. As a result, integration has been achieved in a growing number of cases without depressing either real-estate values or the cultural standards of neighborhoods. (There is no necessary reason, of course, why it should.) Catholics who take part in an "Operation Understanding" of this kind or join in similar efforts to foster good interracial relations are doing no more than their Christian and civic duty. In this respect, the work of the Catholic Interracial Council Movement, founded by the late Father John LaFarge, has been outstanding.

It need scarcely be added that laws forbidding racial dis-

crimination in housing and public accommodations are completely in accord with Catholic teaching both on human rights
and on the nature of property. In enacting such laws, public
authorities are merely discharging their obligation to determine
in detail, when the natural law itself does not do so, the social
duties of private ownership.

CHAPTER 4

Wages and Justice

In contemporary society, the income that puts meat and potatoes on the family table, meets the rent or the mortgage payment, pays the doctor and schoolteacher is derived from several sources. It comes from capital in the form of dividends and interest, from ownership of businesses and farms in the form of proprietors' income, from land in the form of rent, from government insurance systems in the form of unemployment compensation, old-age benefits, and other so-called transfer payments. Finally, it comes from the labor of body and mind in the form of wages and salaries.

For the vast majority of Americans, wages and salaries are the main source of personal income. For many, they are the only source. In 1962, for instance, wage and salary payments, with certain other types of labor income, amounted to $309.2 billion. That was nearly three fourths of total personal income of $442.1 billion. By contrast, rental income of persons amounted to only $12.0 billion, and dividends and interest together to no more than $46.6 billion.

In applying the yardstick of justice to a modern economy, wages are clearly, then, of the highest moment. Historically, the efforts of workers to raise wages in the face of a strong employer resistance embittered the whole transition to an industrial society. Even today, though job security has gained in importance as a divisive element in collective bargaining, wages remain a main cause of industrial disputes.

I

During the nineteenth century, two wage theories were dominant. According to the proponents of economic liberalism, the price of labor, like the price of money, or land, or raw materials, was determined by the operation of the law of supply and demand. The worker was free to accept or reject the market price for his labor. If he accepted it and contracted to work for an employer, the latter was thought to have discharged his full moral obligation to the worker by paying the wage stipulated in the contract.

According to David Ricardo and other early nineteenth-century economists, the market price of labor would always tend toward the subsistence level. Wages would be sufficient only to provide the bare necessities of life. If they fell below that level, population would decline, fewer workers would be available, and wages would rise. But wages would not long remain above the subsistence level, for at that higher level the number of workers would increase and the law of supply and demand would turn against them. After a while, wages would again sink to the subsistence level. This was the so-called Iron Law of Wages.

Economists have long since abandoned the Iron Law of Wages, but it lasted long enough to help spawn Marxist socialism. On the basis of Ricardo's thinking, Karl Marx concluded that the lot of workers in a system of laissez-faire capitalism was hopeless. They could look forward only to a future of increasing misery. The whole wage system, he argued, was unjust. All value is produced by labor and the total product should go, therefore, to the workers. Under the capitalist system, he claimed, owners exploit workers by taking from them (in the form of profits, interest, rent) the "surplus value" of their product, that is, the difference between the market value of the product and the price of labor (wages) that went into it. He concluded, logically enough on his premises, that the source of evil lay in private ownership of the means of production.

Pope Leo answered Ricardo and the whole school of liberal economists by rejecting the commodity concept of labor; he answered the Marxists by denying that labor is the sole source of value, and that the wage contract is, as a consequence, essentially unjust. In so doing, the Pope did not formulate a rival theory of wages. Rather he emphasized certain moral criteria which every wage system that professes to be fair and just has to take into account.

The starting point of Pope Leo's doctrine on wages is a concept of work derived from a study of human nature as God created it. Work is both *personal*, because the energy expended on a job belongs entirely to the worker, and *necessary*, because the product of a man's labor is needed for the preservation of his life. Insofar as work is personal, a man is free to labor for an inhuman, sweatshop wage, or for no wage at all. But insofar as work is necessary, a man is not free morally to accept a wage inadequate to support himself. If he does so, he is failing in the grave duty, incumbent on all men, to preserve the life God gave him.

The nature of human work imposes a condition, therefore, that modifies freedom of contract as it was understood by the economic liberals. Pope Leo explains this:

> Let it be granted, then, that worker and employer may enter freely into agreements and, in particular, concerning the amount of the wage; yet there is always underlying such agreements an element of natural justice, and one greater and more ancient than the free consent of the contracting parties, namely, that the wage shall not be less than enough to support a worker who is thrifty and upright. If, compelled by necessity or moved by fear of a worse evil, a worker accepts a harder condition, which, although against his will, he must accept because the employer or contractor imposes it, he certainly submits to force, against which justice cries out in protest (RN, n. 63).

"It is shameful and inhuman," the Pope had said earlier, "to use men as things for gain and to put no more value on them than what they are worth in muscle and energy" (n. 31).

Nobody today defends the commodity concept of labor. In this respect, American law commendably reinforces the natural law and the Christian view of man. The Clayton Act, which Congress enacted in 1914 for the express purpose of exempting trade unions from certain antimonopoly provisions of the Sherman Antitrust Act, declares flatly that "the labor of a human being is not a commodity or an article of commerce."

Similarly, after several dreary decades during which a majority of the U. S. Supreme Court followed the principles of economic liberalism, a more correct legal concept of freedom of contract came to prevail. In 1905, the Supreme Court ruled (Lochner v. New York) that a state could not abridge the "freedom" of a baker to contract to work more than ten hours a day and sixty hours a week. In 1923, it decreed (Adkins v. Children's Hospital) that the District of Columbia was powerless to prevent women from "freely" working for sweatshop wages. But these and other "laissez-faire" decisions were reversed more than a quarter century ago. Since March 29, 1937, when the court decided that the states did after all have the sovereign power to set minimum wages (West Coast Hotel Company v. Parrish), it has been accepted constitutional doctrine in this country that government possesses adequate authority to protect the weak and powerless from exploitation. The freedom of contract criticized by Pope Leo is no longer an acceptable legal defense of wage injustice.

In 1938, Congress responded constructively to the change in thinking on the Supreme Court. It passed the Fair Labor Standards Act, which establishes minimum wages for workers engaged in interstate commerce and stipulates that they are to be paid at overtime rates for all hours worked beyond eight in a day and forty in a week. Over the years, the coverage of the law has been gradually extended until today most nonfarm workers in interstate commerce enjoy this modest protection of their working standards. Farm workers, including many migrants who follow the harvest from one region to another, must still, unfortunately, take their chances with the law of supply and demand. So must most of the employees of businesses engaged in purely intrastate commerce. It is a "freedom" which they would willingly surrender.

Pope Pius XI's treatment of wage justice reflects both the development of Catholic social science after the appearance of *Rerum Novarum* and the growing interest of economists, following the worldwide depression of the 1930's, in the relationship between wage levels and prosperity.

After *Rerum Novarum* appeared, some doubt arose about the exact meaning of a living wage. Is it a wage sufficient only to support a worker himself, or does it cover the needs of his family as well? Pope Pius XI settled the question with finality. "In the first place," he wrote, "the worker must be paid a wage sufficient to support himself and his family." Pope Pius conceded that it is entirely proper that each member of the family should contribute, according to his capacity, to its support. But he denounced child labor and the forced employment of mothers outside the home. It is an "intolerable abuse," he said, "that mothers should be obliged to engage in gainful occupations, to the neglect of household duties, because of the father's low wages. Every effort must therefore be made that fathers of families receive a wage large enough to meet ordinary family needs adequately" (QA, n. 71).

In *Divini Redemptoris*, Pope Pius XI gives perhaps the best description in papal literature of what a living wage means in contemporary society:

> But social justice cannot be said to have been satisfied so long as working men are denied a wage that enables them to provide proper sustenance for themselves and for their families; so long as they are denied the opportunity of acquiring a modest fortune and forestalling the plague of universal pauperism; so long as they cannot make suitable provision, through public or private insurance, for periods of illness and unemployment (n. 52).

Pope John echoed this teaching with forceful simplicity when he said that, according to justice and equity, workers should be paid a wage which allows them to live a truly human life and to face up with dignity to their family responsibilities (cf. MM, n. 71).

II

Up to this point, probably nobody would quarrel with the moral argument for a family living wage. After all, men have to live, and are entitled to live in circumstances befitting their dignity as creatures of God. Furthermore, they can live, as Pope Leo noted, only by gaining access to natural resources. For all those, therefore, whose only access to natural resources is a wage, that wage must be sufficient to support life. Justice cannot be satisfied with less.

Furthermore, the work for which wages are a compensation assumes a special dignity when viewed through Christian eyes.

In the civilization of the ancient world, which was based on slavery, manual work was regarded as degrading. With the coming of Christianity, there began a change which is still operative in our times. Not only did St. Joseph labor as a carpenter to support the Holy Family, but the Master Himself did not disdain to follow His foster father's trade. Thus manual labor was divinely dignified. Although the onerous aspect of work remains as a punishment for original sin — "In the sweat of your brow you shall eat bread" reads Genesis — we now see clearly that the labor of a human being has a positive, ennobling character. Through work, man develops his capacities, practices charity by serving his fellowman, and even participates in some sense in the creative work of God. Work is truly a vocation, therefore, by which men merit, with the help of God's grace, an eternal reward.

From this consideration, we gain some idea of how displeasing it must be to God to see human labor unjustly compensated. We can also see, incidentally, how displeasing it must be to Him to see work carelessly or dishonestly performed.

Justice may demand more, of course, than a living wage. The worker's part of the wage contract, namely, the offering of an honest day's work, often represents a contribution to production that is worth more than a mere living wage. Where this is true, the employer is obliged to compensate the worker accordingly. In a country like ours, one may assume in practice that the wage determined by collective bargaining between employers and unions roughly satisfies the demands of justice.

Since work, however, like property, has a social as well as an individual aspect, workers and employers must take the well-being of the whole economy into account in arriving at their wage agreements. "The amount of pay," said Pope Pius XI, "must be adjusted to the public economic good." And he continued:

> Hence, it is contrary to social justice when, for the sake of personal gain and without regard for the common good, wages are excessively raised or lowered; and this same social justice demands that wages be so managed, through agreement of plans and wills, insofar as can be done, as to offer to the greatest possible number the opportunity of getting work and obtaining suitable means of livelihood (QA, n. 74).

In *Mater et Magistra*, Pope John makes the same point. In determining a just wage, he says, due regard must be had not only for the worker's output and the condition of the enterprise, but also for "the demands of the national interest, especially with respect to any impact on employment of the total labor force" (n. 71).

In most of the developed countries of the free world, governments are attempting, "through agreement of plans and wills," to establish a wage policy, as well as a policy for other types of income, that will promote balanced economic growth and a high level of employment. It is widely accepted that no repetition of the disastrous depression of the 1930's or of the severe inflation of the postwar era can be allowed to happen. Toward this end the United States, through a price-support program, as well as in other ways, has been trying for several decades now to maintain a balance between agricultural and industrial prices and income. More recently, it has attempted, by relating pay to productivity (which is defined as output per man-hour of work), to establish noninflationary wage guidelines. All such efforts, despite inevitable imperfections in planning and execution, are deserving of praise and support. Under contemporary conditions, it is only by such conscious measures that the economy can reach its goal, namely, in the words of Pius XI, the supplying of "all the goods and services which the wealth and resources of nature, technical achievement and the social organization of economic life can furnish" (QA, n. 75).

Pope Pius' treatment of wages offers a good example of the Church's teaching that the direction of the economy cannot be left to the forces of competition alone. Human intelligence, guided by the virtues of justice and charity, has a key role to play. In discharging this role, human intelligence does not repeal the law of supply and demand; it uses it, adapts it, to secure the goals of the economy. By this means, ownership and work fulfill their social functions without ceasing to be the activities of private individuals. Private enterprise and public order are reconciled. This is a development in the capitalistic system which Karl Marx did not foresee.

III

So much, then, for the principles of wage justice. Reducing them to practice is another matter, as Pope John XXIII observed, in a wider context, in *Mater et Magistra:*

> The transition from theory to practice is of its very nature difficult. This is notably true when one tries to reduce to concrete forms the Church's social doctrine. And no wonder, in view of the deep-rooted selfishness of human beings, the materialism that pervades so much of modern society and the difficulty of determining the demands of justice in particular cases (n. 229).

Specifically, what happens when employers are financially unable to pay just wages?

The author of *Quadragesimo Anno* distinguishes two cases. In the first, the employer's inability to pay arises from the inefficiency of his operation. In the second, it stems from circumstances, such as unfair competition, that are beyond his personal control.

With regard to the inefficient employer, Pope Pius says that his lack of initiative and energy, or his indifference to technological progress, "must not be regarded as a just reason for reducing the compensation of his workers" (n. 72). He may have to reduce wages to avoid bankruptcy, but the obligation to pay what he owes remains.

In the second case, employers and workers should strive together to remove the unjust obstacles to a profitable operation. In this endeavor, they have a right to expect the help of government. (In some of these unfortunate cases, the decision must be faced whether or not the business ought to be continued.) It happens not infrequently in this country that workers go to the aid of stricken employers. Sometimes they lend money to an employer who has lost his credit rating. Sometimes they accept a temporary reduction of wages. Sometimes, through their union, they furnish technical assistance, as is the practice in the garment industry in New York. Such collaboration is obviously commendable.

The problem of the family wage deserves special consideration. Employers abroad, notably in France and Belgium, made some attempts before World War I, either individually or as members of an industry group, to adjust "the pay for work to family burdens," and for this Pope Pius XI highly praised them (QA, n. 71). From these early efforts arose the family allowance systems which exist today in all the industrialized countries except the United States. Under these systems, the government pays to parents monthly, sometimes out of general tax revenues, sometimes out of funds financed by a tax on payrolls, a sum of money for the support of all children beyond the first or second. The payment is made without regard to need, and parents are free to spend the money as their good judgment and the love they bear their children suggest.

Family allowances appear to be a recognition of the impracticality of family wages in a modern economy. If workers had to be paid not only on the basis of what they produced but also in proportion to the number of children they had, employers would be in no hurry to hire fathers of large families. To do so would put them at a competitive disadvantage with rivals who might find, or invent, all kinds of reasons for employing only single men or fathers of small families. Although this difficulty could possibly be resolved by an industry-wide approach to family allowances, with each employer contributing a percentage of his payroll to a common fund, an answer would still have to be found to the problem of low-wage industries. In some cases these industries are scarcely able to pay a wage sufficient to support the worker himself in decency. A national system of some kind seems to be the only practical solution.

While a few groups in this country, for instance the National Catholic Conference on Family Life, have favored a family-allowance system, the proposal lacks popular and political appeal. Industry hasn't been interested, and neither have the trade unions. Perhaps the fact that wages are relatively high in the United States makes the need for family allowances appear less pressing than it is elsewhere. It should be noted, however, that the federal tax system, by granting exemptions for dependents, does take family burdens into account; so, too, in a limited way do American management and labor, since many privately financed health insurance programs cover the worker's family as well as the worker himself. Finally, in various ways, state governments partially subsidize the higher education of deserving youngsters, as does the federal government. Perhaps the school lunch program and public housing for low-income families may also be considered partial substitutes for a system of family allowances.

None of these programs for supplementing the wages of workers should be regarded as socialistic. After referring, in *Casti Connubii*, an encyclical on marriage, to the duty of employers to pay a family living wage, Pope Pius XI added:

If, however, private resources do not suffice for this, it is the duty of the public authority to supply for the insufficiency of personal effort; particularly in a matter which is of such importance to the commonweal, touching as it does the maintenance of the family and married people.

Those who are too quick to equate social reform with socialism make a bigger contribution to the spread of Marxism than they realize. Catholics who do so are plainly ignorant of the social teaching of their Church.

IV

Like a number of other leaders who have seriously sought an end to industrial conflict, Pope Pius XI recommended liberalizing the wage contract. Although he insisted just as strongly as Pope Leo that the wage contract is not "unjust of its nature," he saw, if not the need, at least the practical wisdom of incorporating in it features of a partnership contract. He wrote in *Quadragesimo Anno:*

> We consider it more advisable, however, in the present condition of human society that, so far as is possible, the work contract be somewhat modified by a partnership contract, as is already being done in various ways and with no small advantage to workers and owners. Workers and other employees thus become sharers in ownership or management, or participate in some fashion in the profits earned (n. 65).

We have already seen, in the preceding chapter, that Pope John vigorously supported this proposal (cf. MM, nn. 76, 91–93), as did Pope Pius XII in several of his allocutions (To Catholic Employers, May 7, 1949; To the International Congress of Social Study, June 3, 1950).

For a long time the American labor movement was suspicious of profit sharing and stock ownership (just as employers have been, and largely remain, suspicious of sharing in management). It tended to see in these proposals an employer strategy to avoid paying honest wages and to weaken the attachment of workers to their union. Since World War II, however, there has been a striking change in labor's thinking. Today, even such a militant union as the United Auto Workers is willing to negotiate contracts with a profit-sharing clause. While sharing in profits and ownership may not be practical in many cases, and should certainly not be regarded as a panacea for all industrial ills, it could lead, if widely enough practiced, to a more equitable distribution of industrial income. Its spread over the past few decades — from 109 profit-sharing plans in 1930 to about 35,000 in 1962 — is one of the more heartening developments in the postwar American scene. Toward this growth the Council of Profit Sharing Industries, which insists, as a matter of principle, that profit sharing must be an addition to, not a substitute for, fair wages, has made a valuable contribution.

At the present time, profit sharing is receiving an unexpected boost from the world competitive situation. With the recovery of Western Europe and Japan from the ravages of World War II, many American firms have found it increasingly difficult to retain their foreign markets and to resist invasions of the domestic market. Since American wage rates are notably higher than those abroad — even after allowance is made for the relatively larger role "fringe" benefits play in Japan and several European countries — there is strong pressure in such industries as steel and automobiles to resist wage increases. As a result, unions are becoming more interested than formerly in the possibilities of profit sharing or sharing in cost savings, since these methods of compensation increase worker income without putting pressure on prices. Recent experiments along these lines at Kaiser Steel and American Motors seem very promising.

The problem that international trade presents to students of wage justice was familiar to Pope Leo XIII, at least in its broad scope. The question arose toward the end of the nineteenth century when several European governments were striving, very belatedly, to improve the lot of their workers. They quickly discovered that because of trade across national frontiers they could not do very much to reform their industrial practices unless other competing nations made similar efforts. In 1889, as a result of a campaign conducted by Gaspard Decurtins, a pioneer Catholic social reformer, Switzerland invited other European countries to an international conference on labor legislation. Eventually the meeting was held in Berlin in 1890, with the Bishop of Breslau in attendance as the representative of the Holy See. Pope Leo confirmed his approval of the project, which may be said to have prepared the way for the founding of the International Labor Organization after World War I, by writing to Mr. Decurtins in 1893:

> It is clear to anyone that the protection given to the workers would be imperfect if it were afforded only by the different laws which each country has passed on its own account. For since commodities coming from various countries enter into the same market, the regulation of conditions of labor imposed here or there would result in the industrial products of one nation expanding to the detriment of another (quoted in Lewis Watt, S.J., A Handbook to Rerum Novarum, p. 58).

Against this background it is easy to understand the sympathy and support which the Holy See has consistently given to the International Labor Organization. Pope John's tribute in Mater et Magistra came as no surprise to those familiar with the history of modern Catholic social thought. His remarks which follow recall the laudatory reference to the ILO in Quadragesimo Anno (n. 22) and the enthusiasm with which Pope Pius XII greeted the ILO Governing Body in an audience at the Vatican in November, 1954:

> We are also happy to express our heartfelt appreciation to the International Labor Organization, which for decades has been making its effective and precious contribution to the establishment in the world of a socioeconomic order marked by justice and humanity and one in which the lawful demands of the workers are recognized and defended (n. 103).

Ever since 1919, the ILO has striven, with the cooperation of most of its member governments, to elevate labor standards all over the world. Were it not for the progress that has been made in carrying out ILO recommendations on minimum wages, unemployment compensation, hours of work, protective measures for women and children, trade-union rights, and a number of other matters, all having implications for production costs, the competitive position of American industry would be more unfavorable than it actually is. The desirable answer to international disparity in wage rates and working conditions is not to depress American standards, but to raise standards elsewhere. It is a hopeful sign that in recent years wage rates have been rising faster in Japan and some West European countries than they have in the United States.

CHAPTER 5

Fair Shares for All

From a moral standpoint, the true prosperity of a country does not consist solely in the size of its gross national product — in the sum, that is to say, of all the goods and services it produces. It consists even more in an equitable distribution of the national product among all the people. For only when men have adequate material resources can they develop normally as human beings. Pope John expressed this succinctly in *Mater et Magistra*:

> The economic prosperity of a people should be measured, not only in terms of its aggregate wealth, but also and much more in terms of the real distribution of wealth according to the norms of justice. That is, national wealth should be measured according to the degree in which it guarantees the personal development of all the members of society. This, indeed, is the true goal of a national economy (n. 74).

As we have seen in Chapter 2, concern over the maldistribution of wealth and income runs like a theme through all the Church's social teaching. In *Rerum Novarum*, Pope Leo deplored the extremes of affluence and misery in his day, the "abounding wealth among a very small number and destitution among the masses" (n. 1). To Pope Pius XI "the immense multitude of non-owning workers on the one hand and the enormous riches of certain very wealthy men on the other" were an unanswerable argument "that the riches which are so abundantly produced in our age of 'industrialism,' as it is called, are not rightly distributed and equitably made available to the various classes of people" (QA, n. 60). He went on to insist that every effort be made "that at least in the future a just share only of the fruits of production be permitted to accumulate in the hands of the wealthy, and that a sufficiently ample share be supplied to workingmen" (n. 61). Even though the living standards of workers in the advanced countries have notably improved since the 1930's, we find Pope John still insisting that "attentive care must be taken and every effort made that socioeconomic inequalities do not increase but rather are lessened as much as possible" (MM. n. 73).

I

At this point in our study, it is pertinent to consider how successful we have been in distributing the wealth the United States so abundantly produces.

In *Pacem in Terris,* Pope John listed among the basic rights of man the right "to the means which are necessary and suitable for the proper development of life." In addition to food, clothing, shelter, rest and medical care, these means include, he said, the necessary social services: the right of a man "to security in cases of sickness, inability to work, widowhood, unemployment, or in any other case in which he is deprived of the means of subsistence through no fault of his own" (n. 11). To what extent is this basic right guaranteed in the United States? To what extent, in other words, have we been able to reduce poverty, to give all our people a decent livelihood, and to avoid extreme inequalities in income and living standards? To what extent has the goal of a family living wage been realized among us?

These questions are not easy to answer. Right in the beginning, we are faced with the vexing problem of determining in the concrete what poverty is. The concept has a relative aspect that obviously must be taken into consideration. Anyone who has ever seen the slums of the Orient, or of Africa or Latin America, knows that many people considered to be poor in Chicago or New York would be regarded as fairly well off by the masses in the smelly streets of Calcutta or by the refugee shack dwellers on the barren hills of Hong Kong.

In an excellent article in the New York *Times Magazine* (April 21, 1963), Herman P. Miller, of the U. S. Bureau of Census, emphasized this point in describing poverty in stricken Harlan County, Ky. Two thirds of the houses, he wrote, are substandard. Half don't have baths or inside toilets. A quarter even lack running water. Yet 88 percent of the families in those run-down houses have a washing machine, 67 percent have a television set, 45 percent have a telephone, and 59 percent have a car. Are these people poor? Of course they are. By our living standards, not many Americans are much poorer. Yet the comforts and conveniences of a rich society that they possess — even when water for the washing machine must be drawn from a well, and the car is a rickety jalopy — place these people much higher on the totem pole than their counterparts anywhere else in the world.

Most people would agree that poverty is the lack of those goods and services which are considered by the community generally as necessary for a decent human life. For anyone concerned about his neighbor's welfare, it makes no difference that this lack of goods and services differs from country to country, depending on its natural resources and stage of economic development, and even within the same country at different periods in its history. (What are regarded as necessities today would in many cases have been considered comforts and even luxuries a century ago.) It is enough for us to know that our neighbor is ill-fed, ill-clad, ill-housed, insecure — that he is, in a word, poor.

In a money economy, the most practical way to define poverty is in terms of income. This has been done by a number of public and private agencies and individuals.

In a study published by the Congressional Joint Economic Committee in 1959, *The Low Income Population and Economic Growth*, Professor Robert J. Lampman considered a four-person family to be in the "low-income" category if its total money income was not more than $2,500 in 1957 dollars. The corresponding figure for unattached individuals was $1,157.

If for the purpose of obtaining a rough estimate we equate low income with poverty, there were 32.2 million poor Americans in 1957.

Four years later, Dr. Lampman updated his study. Setting the poverty level for a single person at anything less than $1,250 in 1962, and for a family of four at less than $2,700, he estimated the number of poor at 34 million. Professor Lampman considers his poverty-income levels conservative.

The widely discussed analysis by the Conference on Economic Progress, *Poverty and Deprivation in the United States*, which was published in 1962 under the direction of Leon H. Keyserling, assumes that multiperson families with less than $4,000 in 1960 were living in poverty. Mr. Keyserling's cutoff figure for individuals was $2,000. Even after allowance is made for price changes between 1957 and 1960, as well as for such nonmonetary income as food raised and consumed on farms, which Professor Lampman excluded, the CEP figures are considerably higher than those in the Joint Economic Committee study. Mr. Keyserling puts the poor in the United States at 38 million.

Michael Harrington, in his scorching *The Other America: Poverty in the United States*, also uses the $4,000 figure for families and the $2,000 figure for individuals as the poverty dividing line. His estimate of the extent of poverty, though, is higher than Mr. Keyserling's. Between 40 and 50 million Americans are poor, he claims.

It should be noted that these and similar studies of the low-income population use as raw materials the "Current Population Reports" of the Bureau of Census and the income series of the Office of Business Economics of the U. S. Department of Commerce. Since these government bureaus do not offer a definition of poverty, the identification of poverty with any given income level is the responsibility of the respective authors. To afford the reader some basis for an independent judgment, it may be helpful at this point to consider the well-known budget for a city worker's family which the Bureau of Labor

Statistics developed in 1946 at the request of Congress.

The BLS budget, which envisages a family of four — "an employed husband, aged 38, with a wife not employed outside the home, and two children, a girl aged 8 and a boy aged 13" — is neither a minimum subsistence budget, such as a welfare agency might use, nor a luxury budget. Rather it represents a "modest but adequate" level of living according to standards prevailing in the community.

It offers the worker and his family a rented five-room apartment (not counting the bathroom) within ten blocks of public transportation and not adjacent to a refuse dump, railroad tracks, or other nuisance. It supposes that the apartment is suitably furnished and that the worker's wife has a gas or electric stove, a refrigerator (with a frozen-food compartment), a vacuum cleaner, and a washing machine.

The family is allowed nearly 20 quarts of milk, or the equivalent in milk products, a week; about 14 pounds of meat, poultry, and fish; a little more than two dozen eggs (nearly an egg a day per person). It can have 9½ pounds of tomatoes or citrus fruits, and almost a pound of coffee — not to mention 173 cans of beer a year and two bottles of liquor. If they wish, the members of the family are permitted a total of 212 meals a year away from home (mostly lunches for husband at work and children at school.) There is also provision for soft drinks for the children — about 40 ounces a week.

The husband can buy a new suit and hat every two years, and five shirts a year. The wife can shop for 3½ dresses (one a house dress) every year, and a coat and three fifths of a hat every two years.

The budget permits the purchase of a secondhand auto every three years. The family may also have a television set (a new one every nine years), spend $20 a year on books and magazines, and go to the movies once every two weeks. For gifts of all kinds, including contributions to churches and charities, $121 a year is allotted.

It is scarcely necessary to add that the budget makes pro-

vision for medical and dental care. It does not, however, allow
anything for savings.

Before we consider this budget in money terms, a little
history may be instructive. For a seven-year period after 1951,
BLS stopped pricing its budget. The list of goods and services
it covered, which reflected family spending patterns in 1934–
1936 and 1941, had become outdated. By the 1950's, living
standards of urban families had significantly risen over those
prevailing before the war. If the budget was to have meaning
for the 1960's, not only would new items have to be added,
but the quantity and quality of old items would have to be
increased to reflect higher incomes, changed buying habits, and
new community standards. Indeed, an even more thoroughgoing
revision was indicated. Since this could not be accomplished
for several years, BLS decided to publish an "interim" budget
based on prices prevailing in the autumn of 1959. This experience illustrates the relative, changing aspect of poverty
described earlier in this chapter.

In the following table, the BLS estimates are expressed in
1960 dollars:

**"Modest but Adequate" Budget for Four-Person Families in Ten Cities,
1960**

	City	Total Budget	Food and Beverages	Rent, Heat Utilities	Other Goods and Services	Other Costs	Taxes
1.	Atlanta	$5,696	$1,528	$1,162	$2,197	$260	$549
2.	Boston	6,377	1,875	950	2,258	260	732
3.	Chicago	6,629	1,768	1,399	2,493	260	709
4.	Houston	5,421	1,500	950	2,216	260	495
5.	Kansas City	6,021	1,646	1,128	2,365	260	622
6.	Los Angeles	6,345	1,764	1,189	2,423	297	672
7.	New York	6,027	1,870	1,023	2,203	276	655
8.	Pittsburgh	6,258	1,907	1,022	2,386	260	683
9.	Scranton	5,747	1,775	879	2,226	260	607
10.	Washington	6,205	1,700	1,238	2,310	260	697

Under the item "Other Costs" are included life insurance,
social security tax, and such occupational expenses as union dues.
The "modest but adequate" budget studies for unattached

individuals set the requirement within a range from somewhat below $2,300 to a little above $3,000, depending on the city.

In attempting to arrive at conclusions from the BLS budget, other factors besides money income must be taken into account. Place of residence is important: one can live more cheaply in small rural communities than in big cities; in the South than in the North. The size of the family is highly significant, as is the age of its members. For the cities it studied, BLS estimates, for example, that the budget for a four-person family ranges from a low of $5,036 to a high of $7,678, depending on "the age of the head of the family, age of the children, and other family composition factors." For a family of six or more persons, the range is from $6,080 to $9,357. And in all cases, how efficiently a family manages its affairs is extremely important. A wife who is a good cook and seamstress, and who can shop intelligently, makes a notable contribution to a family's standard of living even though she brings in no income.

For the purpose of discussion at least, it seems reasonable to accept the Conference on Economic Progress figures of under $4,000 for the multiperson families and below $2,000 for unattached individuals as indicative of the poverty level in the United States. (There has been a rise in the consumer price level since 1960 but not big enough, as this book goes to press the summer of 1964, to change the picture notably.) Selecting a standard of this kind does not mean, of course, that every family with less than $4,000 is poverty-stricken, or that some families with more than $4,000 may not be poor. Small families in certain parts of the country can manage fairly well on less than $4,000, and on the other hand some large families may be poor even though they have more than $4,000.

In addition to the poverty level, the CEP study explores what it calls the "deprivation" level, a level that "means genuine denial of many of the goods and services which most Americans have come to regard as 'essentials,' and in most cases imposes a continuing sense of insecurity." Families with more than $4,000 but less than $6,000 are said to be living in deprivation. So are individuals with more than $2,000 but less than $3,000.

The table below, as well as the other tables which follow in this chapter, is adapted from studies of the Commerce Department's Office of Business Economics. It shows the number of families and unattached individuals on the lower rungs of the income ladder in 1960.

Personal Income Before Taxes	Families (in thousands)	Individuals (in thousands)
Under $2,000	3,370	3,943
$2,000–$2,999	3,088	2,090
$3,000–$3,999	4,170	1,768
$4,000–$4,999	4,943	1,222
$5,000–$5,999	5,315	683

Thus a total of 10,628,000 families and 3,943,000 unattached individuals were in the poverty-income group. Since there were 45,370,000 family units and 10,680,000 unattached individuals in the country in 1960, this means that 23 percent of all families and 37 percent of all individuals were living in poverty. An additional 10,258,000 families and 2,090,000 individuals, though not poor, were living on the deprivation level. According to the CEP study, there were 77 million Americans in these low-income categories in 1960, 38 million of them in the poverty group.

II

On considering these figures, one might be led to conclude that the American reputation for a high-wage economy is largely mythical. How false such a conclusion would be appears from an analysis of the composition of the lowest income groups.

In an address to the Catholic Economic Association in December, 1961, the late Selma F. Goldsmith, using the Census Bureau's "Current Population Reports," pointed out that of all families with money incomes under $3,000 in 1960 nearly a third were headed by persons 65 years old and over. About a fifth were headed by women (these are the "broken" families). Another fifth were rural-farm families. Taken together, these groups accounted for two thirds of all families with less than $3,000 a year.

In terms of employment status, 41 percent of the low-income families were headed by a person not in the labor force or in the armed services. (Many of these were older families living on social security pensions or other types of retirement income.) In nearly a third of the cases where the head was employed, the jobs were in the service or common labor categories.

Thus it is clear that for one reason or another many low-income families are not active agents in the nation's economic life. When they are, they are heavily concentrated in the low-wage industries. The reasons for this — physical or mental handicaps, lack of education and skills, racial discrimination — are more a sociological than an economic problem. This does not mean that the problem shouldn't trouble our consciences. It should. It means only that poverty can and does coexist with a high-wage economy.

For the United States does have a high-wage economy, if a high-wage economy can be said to exist anywhere in the world. In July, 1963, the average gross weekly earnings per worker in the nation's manufacturing establishments was $99.23. In the durable goods industries, employing nearly 10 million workers, the average wage was $108.09. It was $88.36 in the nondurable goods industries, which had more than 7 million workers on the payroll. In nonmanufacturing establishments, high weekly wages prevailed in mining ($112.34), in contract construction ($130.90), in transportation and public utilities ($101.94). These industries employed another 7 million workers. In some of the service industries, wages were admittedly low — $48.60 in hotels, $51.74 in laundries, $69.30 in retail trade, $74.77 in banking. But they were high in wholesale trade ($99.96) and in insurance ($96.35).

These are all gross figures, before deductions for taxes and social security. They are also average figures: in durable goods, for instance, some workers received more than $108.09 a week, some less. They are weekly figures and, therefore, not always a good indication of annual earnings. On the other hand, they do not include such "fringe" benefits as paid vacations, medical and life insurance, and supplementary unemployment benefits, financed in whole or in part by employers. The value of these benefits frequently amounts to a fifth or more of the weekly wage. All things considered, then, wage statistics present a picture of a high-wage economy.

This is reflected to some extent in the following table, which shows the progress that has been made since prewar days in reducing the size of low-income groups and in expanding the middle-income groups. All the income figures are in 1962 dollars.

Family Income (before taxes)	Families and Unattached Individuals (in millions)		
	1929	1947	1962
Under $2,000	11.2	7.2	7.1
$2,000–$3,999	13.9	12.6	10.9
$4,000–$5,999	5.6	11.7	12.2
$6,000–$7,999	2.4	6.0	10.8
$8,000–$9,999	1.1	3.1	6.7
$10,000 and over	1.9	4.1	10.9
Total	36.1	44.7	58.6

Between 1929 and 1947 the number of families and individuals with incomes below $4,000 fell sharply, from 70 percent of all families and individuals to 46 percent. The decline in the number with incomes below $2,000 was especially gratifying. Since 1947, however, the number of families and individuals with less than $2,000 has remained almost unchanged, though it had fallen relatively from 16 percent of all families and individuals to 12 percent. At the same time there has been a huge growth in the income brackets between $4,000 and $10,000. Half of all American families — many of them families of workers — are in those brackets today. Only a quarter were there in 1929.

The small decline in the number of families and individuals with less than $4,000 during the 15 years between 1947 and 1962 becomes doubly a matter of concern when contrasted with the large bulge in the high-income brackets. In 1962, families and individuals with $10,000 or more a year were nearly a fifth of all families and individuals. They were less than a tenth in 1947. These top-income people receive a disproportionately large share of all family income. This can be seen clearly if we divide all consumer units into five numerically equal groups, called quintiles, and note the share of each in total family income. In the table below, income is computed after taxes.

Quintile	Percentage of Total Income		
	1955	1958	1961
Lowest	5.2	5.0	5.0
Second	11.9	11.6	11.5
Third	17.0	16.8	16.9
Fourth	22.7	22.9	23.0
Highest	43.2	43.7	43.6

The top fifth of U. S. consumer units have a considerably bigger share of total family income than the three lower fifths have together. In this respect, the concentration of income parallels the concentration of ownership noted in Chapter 3. In fact, the concentration becomes even more striking if only the top 5 percent of income receivers — those with incomes of $16,430 and up — are considered. In 1961, this small affluent group of families and individuals received, after taxes, 17.7 percent of all family income.

In a rich country, imbalances in wealth and income are less noticeable, and certainly less productive of discontent and social disorder, than they are in poor countries. But, on moral grounds alone, they are significant in rich countries too. Surely, one can easily doubt that the pattern of income distribution in the

United States satisfies the canons of social justice. During
World War II a trend toward more equitable sharing of the
fruits of production set in, but this was quickly checked. Since
1955, as the table above shows, the percentage shares of the
bottom fifths have slightly declined. That is not a development
which holds promise for a better future.

It appears, furthermore, that the inequality between the
top-income group and the low- and middle-income groups is
understated.

A significant part of the income of many well-to-do families
and individuals escapes measurement. In computing income
shares, the table above ignores, for example, undistributed
corporate profits, which belong to the stockholders, deferred
compensation to corporate executives, which shows up in the
form of liberal retirement plans, and stock options to the same
executives. Not included, either, are realized capital gains and
that portion of business expense accounts which is really a form
of personal income. It is widely believed that since the 1920's
the gulf between the top-income group and those in the low
and middle brackets has sharply narrowed. In support of this,
some cite the fact that whereas in 1929 the top 5 percent on
the income scale had 30 percent of all personal income, it had
only 17.7 percent in 1961. But if income were defined differ-
ently, so as to include the types that now escape measurement,
the picture would be less reassuring.

III

In every free society, where individuals are thrown together
in a competitive economic struggle, a tendency toward gross
inequalities in wealth and income is inevitable. The task of
controlling these imbalances in the interest of social justice
and civic peace, and of reducing them when necessary, is a
never ending one. Here, as elsewhere, eternal vigilance is the
price of liberty.

It is not surprising, then, that one of the sharpest conflicts
in American society today, as in other societies as well, con-

tinues to range around patterns of income distribution. Some of our leading business organizations argue quite frankly that existing inequalities in the distribution of income must become greater before the economy can achieve a higher rate of economic growth. According to them, investment is the key to more and better jobs, and investment depends (1) on savings and (2) on the prospect of profits. But savings in the volume required for significant investments are made only by rich individuals and by corporations (in the form of retained earnings). Therefore, public policy should favor reduction of taxes on large incomes and on corporate profits. Although this policy would permit the rich to become richer, we are assured that it would at the same time benefit the poor. The imbalance between rich and poor would be greater, but the poor would be better off than before.

Opponents of this viewpoint, while not resisting all tax reduction on corporations and high personal incomes, are unwilling to accept a greater degree of inequality as the price of economic progress. With Pope Pius XI, they recognize the legitimacy of profits, since "it is only fair that he who renders service to the community and makes it richer should also, through the increased wealth of the community, be made richer himself . . ." (QA, n. 136). With Pope Pius XII, they understand that overemphasis on the social duties of ownership discourages the enterprising businessman. They would agree with what the Pope, discussing government efforts to bring a measure of security to all classes in society, told the Italian Federation of Commerce on February 17, 1956:

> It is important, however, that the anxious desire for security on the part of the worker should not discourage the businessman's readiness to risk his resources so as to dry up his every creative impulse; nor impose on enterprises operating conditions that are too burdensome; nor discourage those who devote their time and energy to commercial transactions.

But those who refuse to accept wider inequalities as a condition of progress also agree with Pope John XXIII in *Mater et Magistra* that existing socioeconomic inequalities should be lessened rather than widened (cf. n. 73), that taxes ought to be levied according "to the capacity of people to contribute" (n. 136), and that social security systems "can contribute effectively to the redistribution of national income according to standards of justice and equity" (n. 136).

And they agree, finally, with Popes Pius XI and Pius XII that there is, and ought to be, more to the motivation of private enterprise than an all-consuming pursuit of profit. "Expending larger incomes so that opportunity for gainful work may be abundant," said Pope Pius XI, is an outstanding exercise "of the virtue of munificence." And Pope Pius XII, in the address to the Italian businessmen cited above, said that an instinct to "create, to improve and to progress" explains commercial activity as much as, and even more than, the mere desire for gain.

No one denies the essential relationship of savings and investment to economic progress. Certainly the Popes do not. But they do not believe that saving and investment should be restricted to a tiny, affluent minority. That is why Pope Leo insisted on wages high enough to permit frugal workers to amass savings. That is why Pope Pius XI recommended that elements of the partnership contract be included in the wage contract. That is why both Pope Pius XII and Pope John appealed to the heads of corporations that finance their expansion mostly from depreciation allowances and retained profits to permit employees to acquire a share in ownership.

IV

While a just wage system must remain the chief means of bringing about a fair distribution of family income, it has limitations, as was explained in Chapter 4, that seem insuperable. Wages in the United States will not be related to family burdens in the foreseeable future. It is true that unions talk about family needs, but in practice the family they have in mind is a "typical" family of four. That is why they are satisfied to negotiate a flat wage, which is the same for all their members, whether these have a dozen children or none at all.

If we use the BLS budget for a four-person urban family as a guideline, we can set a living wage for small families living in cities somewhere between $5,000 and $6,500 a year. Millions of American workers make that much, and more. But other millions don't. If family incomes are higher in this country than wage rates indicate they should be, the reason is that in many households there is more than one wage earner, or that in many others the single wage earner performs two jobs. In the spring of 1963, nearly a third of all Americans in the labor force were women. More than half of these were married. Then, too, many younger workers, both male and female, live at home and assume their share of family expenses. Furthermore, according to Labor Department estimates, more than four million Americans are holding two jobs or, as the saying goes, are "moonlighting." These extra incomes contribute significantly to the relatively high living standards of many working-class families.

No doubt, there are men who can do a full day's work and then take on a part-time job without injuring their health or neglecting their families, just as there are married women who can successfully combine outside work with housekeeping; but surely moonlighting and the participation of so many married women in the work force — about 40 percent of them with children under 18 — are not acceptable answers to the moral demand for a family living wage.

Incidentally, in the vast majority of cases where wives work, there is a husband in the home. That raises the question: Why do so many married women work?

In a pamphlet published a quarter century ago, *Women in Industry*, the Social Action Department, N.C.W.C., said that the answer is simple: "They work because they must."

Studies made in more recent times tend to confirm that conclusion. They show that some women work because they are interested in a career, or are bored at home, or enjoy the independence a job gives them, or desire a higher standard of living for their families. They also show, however, that in the majority of cases they work to support themselves or to help support dependents. According to the Census Bureau of the U. S. Department of Commerce, most of the married women in the labor force in 1956 came from homes where the husband earned $5,000 a year or less.

As a practical matter, in addition to profit sharing and wider participation in ownership, the solution to adequate family incomes, as well as to a more equitable distribution of income, lies in a more extensive and realistic use of the insurance principle. Over the past quarter century, considerable progress has been made, on both the public and private level, in giving the masses of our people some protection against the hazards of joblessness, disability, and old age. The benefits under public insurance programs should be revised upward both to compensate for inflation and to respond more adequately to family needs. In only a few states, for instance, do unemployment compensation systems make any provision for the children of jobless workers. And eventually, besides a better and more extensive system of health insurance, we shall have to consider the need for family allowances. Without such allowances, millions of workers in the richest country of the world will never enjoy the equivalent of a family living wage.

CHAPTER 6

Government and Economic Life

Ever since the first administration of President Franklin D. Roosevelt, the role of government in society has been one of the great issues in American political life. Time and again, as government expanded to cope with problems at home and crises abroad, voices have been heard in the land warning that the nation is headed toward the dreary wasteland of socialism. On the other hand, one of the most widely read economists of our generation, John Kenneth Galbraith, eloquently argued in *The Affluent Society* that the public sector of the economy has been slighted, and that unless government spends a bigger share of the national product than it is now spending, the growing gulf betwen private affluence and public poverty will have the most disastrous social consequences.

The issues raised by this controversy interest many people — economists, sociologists, political scientists. They also interest theologians and moral philosophers. That this is so should not seem strange or surprising, since a little reflection will show that a man's conception of the role of government is importantly determined by his deepest beliefs about human beings, their purpose in life and the society in which they work out their destiny.

How true this is can readily be seen from the reactions of people to the issue of big government. Men who believe that the individual human being doesn't count for much and are prepared to subordinate him to the progress of a particular class or race or nation tend to regard government bigness as a positive good. Similarly, those who exalt the individual in the spirit of eighteenth-century liberalism are instinctively led to oppose expansion of government power. So it is that our native collectivists are delighted with developments over the past three decades and are disappointed only that government expansion hasn't gone much further than it has; whereas the economic liberals in our midst are dismayed by the trend of events and sigh nostalgically for the good old days of President McKinley and laissez faire.

Between these extremes stands a third group which lacks an appropriate ideological label. Like the economic liberals, they have a high regard for the individual human being, but unlike the liberals they stress the social as well as the individualistic aspects of human nature. Like the collectivists, they recognize that man must live in society and achieve his perfection as a member of a community, but unlike collectivists they refuse to permit man to be absorbed by society and lose his identity in the human mass.

Stemming from this concept of human nature, which in the Western world is the product of Judeo-Christian culture, is a philosophy of government that can best be described as "middle-of-the-road." While recognizing the state as the supreme political power in society, this philosophy does not accord it unlimited authority. It holds that individuals and families are prior to the state and possess rights independently of it. These rights are "unalienable," as the American Declaration of Independence proclaimed, because they derive from God, the Creator. The state is obliged to respect and protect them. On the other hand, the state is not to be looked upon as a negative factor in society, a kind of necessary evil that resulted from the original sin of Adam. Far from being merely a passive policeman, as economic liberals hold, it is a positive force charged with the duty of defending and promoting the common good.

That is the concept of the state which we find in the Church's social teaching.

I

A generation that has experienced a huge expansion of government and the flowering of the welfare state finds it hard to appreciate that Pope Leo's teaching on the role of public authority was considered radical by many of his contemporaries. Partly because of traditional fear and suspicion of government, partly because the theories of economic liberalism were superficially appealing and those of socialism frightening, a number of European Catholics sided with the noninterventionists in the nineteenth-century debate over the state. They accepted much of the laissez-faire argument that the duties of government were limited to defending the country against foreign attack, to preserving domestic law and order, to guaranteeing enforcement of private contracts, to preventing monopoly, and to furnishing certain facilities and services, such as roads, bridges, harbors, schools, parks, insane asylums, and poorhouses, which offered little prospect of profit to private enterprise. In discharging these duties the state fully performed its function of promoting and safeguarding the common good. It had no right, therefore, to interfere in the economy. Economic society was free and autonomous: it was the exclusive preserve of private enterprise.

Pope Leo accepted the distinction between political and economic society, since the confusion of the two was one of the reasons for his condemnation of socialism. But he rejected the restrictions that the economic liberals placed on the state's pursuit of the common good. More specifically, he vindicated the duty of government to intervene in the economy to protect the rights of citizens and to assure a regime of justice. "If, therefore, any injury has been done to, or threatens, either the common good or the interests of individual groups," he wrote, "which injury cannot in any other way be repaired or prevented, it is necessary for public authority to intervene" (RN, n. 52).

In the circumstances existing in the nineteenth century, this meant that the state should concern itself especially with improving the condition of workers. Not only is their labor essential to the well-being of the community, but they are less able than the rich to look after themselves and defend their interests:

Equity therefore commands that public authority show proper concern for the worker so that from what he contributes to the common good he may receive what will enable him, housed, clothed and secure, to live his life without hardship. Whence it follows that all those measures ought to be favored which seem in any way capable of benefiting the condition of workers. Such solicitude is so far from injuring anyone that it is destined rather to benefit all, because it is of absolute interest to the state that those citizens should not be utterly miserable from whom such necessary goods proceed (n. 51).

What were the miseries under which workers groaned in Leo's time and which the state should remove?

Wherefore, if at any time disorder should threaten because of strikes or concerted stoppages of work . . . if in factories danger should assail the integrity of morals through the mixing of the sexes or other pernicious incitements to sin, or if the employer class should oppress the working class with unjust burdens or should degrade them with conditions inimical to human personality or to human dignity, if health should be injured by immoderate work and such as is not suited to sex or age — in all these cases, the power and authority of the law, but of course within certain limits, manifestly ought to be employed (n. 53).

Forty years later Pope Pius XI was to see in this teaching of Leo XIII both broad approval of early government efforts to abolish the more notorious abuses of capitalism, and encouragement to persist in developing a body of labor law. "A new branch of law," he said approvingly, "wholly unknown to earlier times, has arisen from this continuous and unwearied labor to protect vigorously the sacred rights of workers flowing from their dignity as men and as Christians" (QA, n. 28).

Protective legislation of this kind came tardily to the United States, but today our labor legislation includes factory inspection laws, workmen's compensation laws, wage and hour laws, child labor laws, and a nationwide system of unemployment compensation. It also embraces programs for training physically handicapped workers and workers displaced by the progress of automation.

In defending and even demanding state intervention in the economy, Pope Leo was not making a plea for unlimited government. "It is not right," he taught, "for the state to absorb either the citizen or the family; it is proper that the individual and the family should be permitted to retain their freedom of action so far as this is possible without endangering the common good and without injuring anyone" (n. 52). And after specifying the abuses that the state should prevent or abolish, he carefully noted that "the law ought not to undertake more, nor ought it go further, than the remedy of evils or the removal of danger requires" (n. 53).

The successors of Leo have richly developed this doctrine of responsible but limited government. They have adapted it to the vastly different circumstances of the tumultuous era that began with World War I and whose end no man can yet see or predict.

The line of descent and development can be clearly seen in Pope John's *Mater et Magistra*.

The Pope begins by affirming "that the economy is the creation of the personal initiative of private citizens." It is the result, he says, of "their pursuit of common interests either as individuals or in various associations." He immediately adds, though, appealing to the doctrine of his predecessors, that "public authorities also must play an active role in promoting increased productivity with a view to social progress and the welfare of all citizens." They must direct, stimulate, coordinate and supplement the efforts of private enterprise. And the Pope goes on to appeal to experience ("the evolution of history itself") for confirmation "that there can be no well-ordered and prosperous society unless both private citizens and public authorities unite in contributing to the economy." For in the event that "the state fails to act in economic affairs when it should, or acts defectively, incurable civil disorders are seen to follow." And "where the personal initiative of individuals is lacking, political tyranny appears" (nn. 51–53, 56–58).

II

This general philosophy leaves unresolved, however, the perennial problem of deciding in practice precisely what parts government and private enterprise ought to play in developing and directing the economy.

We have already seen that Pope Leo stressed the rule of proportion as an essential guide in determining the type and extent of government intervention. There should be a close relationship, he said, between the action of the state and the need that called it forth. In *Quadragesimo Anno*, Pope Pius XI described this principle in greater detail and gave it the name by which it is now widely known. He called it the principle of subsidiarity — the principle, that is, which governs state aid (*subsidium*) to the economy for the purpose of achieving a prosperous and just society. This is the way he states it:

> This supremely important principle of social philosophy, one which cannot be set aside or altered, remains firm and unshaken: just as it is wrong to withdraw from the individual and commit to the community at large what private enterprise and endeavor can accomplish, so it is likewise unjust and a gravely harmful disturbance of right order to turn over to a greater society of higher rank functions and services which can be performed by lesser bodies on a lower plane. For a social undertaking of any sort, by its very nature, ought to aid the members of the body social, but never to destroy and absorb them (n. 79).

The lesser bodies which the Holy Father refers to are the numerous groups — trade associations, medical and legal societies, trade unions, farm organizations, scientific, civic and charitable groups — that are part of the structure of contemporary society and are a familiar phenomenon in the United States. The Church teaches that these societies, which are called "private" to distinguish them from the public society headed by the state, should be allowed to handle matters within their competence. Otherwise the state would become so burdened by details that it could not perform efficiently the functions that it alone has the authority and capacity to undertake. The principle of subsidiarity may also be regarded, therefore, as a practical formula for avoiding excessive governmental bureaucratization. In American minds, it evokes memories of Abraham Lincoln's statement that government should do for the people what they cannot do, or do so well, for themselves.

It should be clear from its very wording that the principle of subsidiary function lacks the mathematical precision of a yardstick. It does not automatically and painlessly regulate the relationship between citizens and their government. Of course, the state should not do more than is necessary to prevent or correct a social evil, but how in the concrete are we to judge that the state should go precisely so far and no farther, or that, indeed, it has gone far enough? How are we to decide that individuals can or cannot accomplish some project through their own initiative and resources, or that a private organization can very well do a job which the government proposes to undertake? Can depressed areas, like the coal-mining regions of West Virginia and Pennsylvania and the abandoned textile towns of New England, lift themselves up by their bootstraps, under the leadership of local chambers of commerce and other citizen groups, or do they need government help? Can unions and employers get rid of the evils of racial discrimination without the aid of special laws? Can the American people finance medical care through organized private efforts, like Blue Cross and Blue Shield, or do they need a public subsidy, or even a public program?

All such questions involve practical judgments on a set of existing facts and circumstances, and nothing, alas, is more certain than that equally informed people, confronted with decisions of this kind, can and do come to conflicting conclusions. As Cardinal Léger of Montreal told the 1960 meeting of the Canadian Social Week, "Between the clear principles of morality and their final application, too many judgments of facts, too many technical considerations intervene to permit one always to arrive at certitude." Nevertheless, in the hands of men of goodwill, the principle of subsidiarity offers an invaluable, indeed an indispensable, rule for any government that is intent both on preserving a free society and protecting the common good.

If we isolate the principle of subsidiarity and consider it apart from the body of the Church's teaching on the rights and duties of government, it is possible to see in it a purely restrictive and negative norm of action. Some Catholics have mistakenly done this. Time and again, they have invoked the principle as an argument against the efforts of modern governments to reform the capitalistic system and make it more responsive to the common good.

Fortunately, the Popes themselves, by their specific recommendations of government initiative, have shown how narrow and one-sided this view of subsidiarity is. We have already seen that Pope Leo called for a variety of laws to protect workers against exploitation. Pope Pius XI emphasized the need of controlling competition and curbing huge concentrations of industrial and financial power (cf. QA, nn. 88, 110). He also stressed the duty of the state to regulate the use of private property in the interest of the common good (cf. n. 49), to strive to abolish class conflict (cf. n. 81) and to come to the aid of families in need (cf. CC, n. 123). Pope Pius XII spoke of the state's duty to provide jobs when private enterprise fails to do so (cf. Christmas Message, 1952). And in *Mater et Magistra*, Pope John specifies a dozen or more ways in which government ought to intervene in the economy. Worthy of special notice is his treatment of the postwar programs of many governments to cope with the boom-bust cycle (the fatal weakness of an uncontrolled capitalistic system), to assure high levels of production and employment, and to correct the economic imbalances that are the inevitable result of the operations of a free market.

Pope John begins by noting the gains that have been made in recent years both in knowledge of how an economy operates and in the ability to adapt scientific discoveries to the production of wealth. Because of these advances, he says, governments now possess "far greater capacities than in the past for reducing inequalities among the different sectors of production, among the various regions within the same nation, and among the various peoples of the world." Furthermore, he adds, governments are now able "to control fluctuations in the economy and to bring effective remedies to bear on the problem of mass unemployment."

From these developments, which for the first time in human history hold forth the promise of relative abundance for all, two conclusions necessarily follow. Pope John does not hesitate to draw them. The principle of subsidiarity plainly dictates (1) that governments "undertake a variety of economic activities, at once more vast and more highly organized (than heretofore)," and (2) that to accomplish this it is essential that "they devise suitable structures, programs, means and methods" (MM, n. 54).

That is precisely what modern governments are doing today, including the U. S. government. They are striving in various ways — through public works, technical assistance, encouragement to private enterprise — to aid backward areas within their national boundaries. They are striving to speed the economic development of poor countries. They are attempting to "manage" the economic cycle, to avoid violent swings from deep depression to feverish prosperity, and back again. They are intent on promoting a healthy rate of economic growth, with a view to achieving full production and employment along with price stability.

Obviously these are all highly desirable and even necessary objectives. Just as obviously these objectives can only be attained by a certain degree of government initiative and control.

Not that Pope John believed, any more than did Popes Leo and Pius XI, that universal well-being is to be expected from the state (cf. QA, n. 78). He had already insisted, as we have seen, that "the economy is the creation of the personal initiative of private citizens," and before completing his treatment of private enterprise and state intervention, he emphasized again that the result of government intervention ought to be an increase in personal liberty (cf. n. 55). Nevertheless, he was determined to show that the principle of subsidiarity, as the Church understands it, does not inhibit governments from mobilizing their resources to achieve necessary social goals.

III

With reference to the United States, this means that one can find justification in the Church's social teaching not merely for welfare legislation, such as the Social Security Act, or for such regulatory laws as the Interstate Commerce Act, the Securities Exchange Act, or the Pure Food and Drug Act, all of which place limits on private enterprise. It means also that one can find ample warrant for the pathfinding Employment Act of 1946, which empowers the federal government to maintain a policy of promoting "maximum employment, production and purchasing power."

When the Employment Act was approved by a bipartisan vote in Congress, it constituted a formal, sweeping recognition that competition alone, as Popes Leo XIII and Pius XI had said, could not be the sole regulating principle of the nation's economic life. It was a public acknowledgment that the play of competitive forces, while useful and valuable within limits, was unable to prevent wild fluctuations in production, employment, and prices, or to assure a fair distribution of the national product, or to provide the minimum security required for healthy family life. The Employment Act of 1946 committed government, not to a planned economy on the Soviet model, in which the state regulates production and fixes prices and wages, but to economic planning within a democratic framework. It formalized a new relationship between government and private enterprise, one designed to end the divorce brought about by the theory and practice of economic liberalism without at the same time subjecting private enterprise to the suffocating embrace of the state. This new relationship, which can best be described

as cooperative, is still in process of development. It has pro-
ceeded further in most West European countries than in the
United States.

All this will appear novel and dangerous only to those who,
as was said earlier, regard the state as a necessary evil, and who
imagine, as a result, that a hostile relationship between private
enterprise and government is natural, inevitable and praise-
worthy. Such a highly individualistic, almost anarchic view of
government has no basis in the Church's social teaching.

The sharpness of the political struggle in the United States
tends to obscure a broad consensus on the substance of the
interventionist legislation passed during and after the watershed
years of the New Deal. Only on the premise that such a consensus exists can we explain why, during the eight years of the
Eisenhower Administration, no effort was made to repeal any
of this legislation. (In several respects, it was expanded.) None
is likely to be made in the future, although a small but vocal
minority remains highly dissatisfied.

The controversy today, when it is not sheer political rivalry,
rages around either the conduct of public programs or their
size. The "outs" argue that they could do a better job than
the "ins," or that selected government operations could be
reduced in scope or even discontinued. The charge is often made
that government, especially the federal government, is too big,
that it taxes and spends too much, that in the interest of
personal freedom it should be de-emphasized. Guided by our
moral principles, what are we to think of this controversy?

IV

A study of this kind can conveniently start with an analysis
of government budgets, since these reveal not merely how
much government spends but what it spends it for. They also
show the size and origin of government revenues. All the figures
that follow are taken from the national income and product
accounts as tabulated by the Commerce Department's Office
of Business Economics. This budgetary approach relates gov-

ernment expenditures and receipts to the national economy in a more meaningful way than does the administrative budget that the President sends to Congress every January.

Admittedly, the grand total of government spending is impressive. In the calendar year 1962, the federal government spent $109.8 billion; state and local governments, $58.7 billion. After allowing for duplication — an item of $7.6 billion is counted twice, once when given in the form of grants-in-aid by the federal government and again when spent by state and local governments — this makes a total of approximately $161 billion.

Before considering how all this money was spent, let us look briefly at the receipts side of the coin. In 1962, the federal government collected $105.9 billion from individuals and corporations; state and local governments collected $51.4 billion. (These totals, it is worth noting, include $23.9 billion in the form of contributions by individuals and business firms to social insurance programs administered by federal, state, and local governments.) Of all government receipts, personal tax and nontax payments accounted for considerably more than a third, or nearly $58 billion. Taxes on corporate profits brought in $22 billion, and sales and excise taxes $25 billion. Property taxes, in which the federal government has no share, topped $19 billion. These taxes were paid in a country with a national income of $453.7 billion.

So much, then, for the overall picture of the income flow from citizens to their government.

How did government spend $161 billion in 1962? The table on page 82 tells the story in broad outline.

So far as type of spending goes, we can exclude immediately as noncontroversial the categories of National Defense, General Government, International Affairs and Finance, and Veterans Services and Benefits. These functions and programs fall within the traditional province of government. One can argue that government is spending too much in these fields, but not that it shouldn't be spending at all. These are obviously not

Spending by Type of Function, 1962

(Billions of Dollars)

National Defense	$ 55.5
General Government	18.4
International Affairs and Finance.	2.5
Health, Education, and Welfare.	62.0
Veterans' Services and Benefits.	5.8
Commerce and Housing.	15.8
Agriculture and Argicultural Resources.	5.0
Natural Resources	3.6
Total	$168.6
Subtract for duplication.	7.6
Total	161.0

functions which individuals, acting alone or in groups, are able to perform themselves. But spending in these areas — some $82 billion — accounted for more than half of all government expenditures in 1962. Indeed, close to 40 percent of all government spending — and nearly 60 percent of federal spending — went to pay the cost of past wars and preventing a future war. And that does not include any of the interest on the public debt, much of which was war-incurred.

Scarcely less controversial are a number of programs under Health, Education, and Welfare and under Commerce and Housing. On civilian safety — police, fire, prisons — government spent $4.1 billion; on transportation — highways, water, and air — $11 billion; on public health and sanitation, $7.5 billion; on postal services, $785 million. That adds up to $22.6 billion and brings the total noncontroversial spending — by reason of function, let us repeat — to $104.6 billion. That leaves only $56.4 billion for closer inspection.

It scarcely seems necessary to delay very long on government spending on education, public utilities (local transit, gas, and electricity), and agriculture.

Something like a consensus exists today that government must supplement the efforts of parents to educate their children by providing free public schooling at least on the primary level and probably on the high school level as well. (In the United States, for reasons that are too complex to be explained here, this consensus does not extend to parents who exercise their constitutional right to send their children to religiously oriented schools. In addition to financing a religious school system, which meets all the educational requirements of government authorities, they are obliged to pay taxes to support public schools.) Limited aid to higher education is also generally accepted as a legitimate government activity. In 1962 the bill for government education programs came to $21.6 billion, with local government units spending most of the money.

Similarly, few people are prepared today to pick an ideological fight over government ownership of local public utilities. Spending in this sector amounted to $3.5 billion.

As for agriculture, it is, under modern conditions, a vexing problem for practically every country in the world. Although a minority of Americans argues for a return to a free market in farm products, the vast majority is persuaded that this is not possible. It is noteworthy that in this area, while exhorting farmers to organize for self-help, Pope John called for government assistance of many kinds (cf. MM, nn. 123–141). Even if one concedes that present farm programs should be criticized on a number of counts, it is scarcely arguable that government has no business in this field. In 1962, the cost of government services to agriculture came to $5 billion.

Thus, total spending on education, public utilities, and agriculture amounted to $26.7 billion.

In considering the remaining $29.7 billion of government outlays in 1962, we come finally to two sizable programs that over the years have been hotly debated. The first involves the efforts of government to deal with poverty and hardship; the second, with its activities in the field of natural resources. Together these programs cost $27.8 billion, with public assistance, jobless benefits, old age and retirement benefits accounting for nearly 90 percent of the total.

It would be difficult to prove that under contemporary conditions government welfare and social-security programs are an unjustified incursion into a sector reserved to individuals and private groups. Certainly, Pope John did not condemn them in *Mater et Magistra*. On the contrary, he not only insisted that farmers, despite small contributions to social-security systems, should receive benefits equal to those enjoyed by other groups, but also pointed out that these systems "can contribute effectively to the redistribution of national income according to standards of justice and equity" (MM, nn. 135–136). His whole temperate discussion of socialization, which embraces public as well as private activities, is also pertinent to the question (cf. nn. 59–67). So also is his flat statement in *Pacem et Terris* that a human being has the right to security in cases of sickness, inability to work, widowhood, old age, unemployment, or in any other case in which he is deprived of the means of subsistence through no fault of his own (cf. n. 11).

So far as natural resources go, the only controversy of any note concerns the government's part in the development of water resources. Even here the argument is limited to power development. It does not touch irrigation or flood and river control.

V

Up to this point, the emphasis has been placed on the right and duty of government to perform the type of function that it is discharging. This leaves open the question whether government is overplaying its role, whether it is attempting to do too much and, as a consequence, imposing an excessive tax burden on individuals and businesses. Nothing is more common than to hear businessmen contending that the nation's growth rate would be automatically stepped up if corporations and individuals were free to spend more of their incomes on producer and consumer goods. And in similar vein, some people lament what they describe as the declining freedom of individuals to provide for themselves and their families. If these complaints are justified, there would be grave reason for apprehension, since, as we have seen, the economy should be "the creation of the personal initiative of private citizens."

With regard to the repressive effects of high taxes on economic growth rates, one can say only that experts in the field are divided. Although many agree with the Kennedy and Johnson administrations that lower tax rates would stimulate economic expansion, others are doubtful. In 1953, a study made at the Harvard Business School (*Effects of Taxation: Investments by Individuals* by J. Keith Butters, Lawrence E. Thompson, Lynn L. Bollinger) concluded that "the accumulation of investable funds by the upper-income classes has been consistently large during the postwar years, despite the existing tax structure, and that individuals with large incomes and substantial wealth continue as a group to hold and invest a large proportion of their funds in equity-type investments" (p. 51).

The truth is, as Roger A. Freeman notes in *Taxes for the Schools*, that on the basis of present data and studies we simply do not know whether or not heavy taxes seriously retard economic growth (cf. p. 89). Studies made in 1959 for the International Cooperation Administration indicate that a number of countries, including West Germany, France, and Italy, impose heavier tax burdens than does the United States (cf. *U. S. News and World Report*, April 13, 1959, pp. 88–89). Yet West Germany, France, and Italy have all experienced higher rates of economic growth than we have. Certainly, onerous taxes have had no observable ill effect on the growth rate of the Soviet Union. On the other hand, some countries with lighter tax burdens than ours have had lower economic growth rates.

Nor is the argument against big government as destructive of freedom and initiative anymore open and shut.

It is true that the vast majority of American workers have some protection against unemployment, industrial accidents, and old age. Does anyone seriously believe that the minimum government safeguards against these hazards is sapping their initiative and corroding their will to support themselves and their families? Although welfare state and cradle-to-grave security have become in some quarters topics of easy wit and angry comment, there is little evidence that American workers are any less intent today on improving their living standards than their fathers and grandfathers were.

Furthermore, despite high taxes, American consumers continue to enjoy more freedom of choice — and therefore more chance to act responsibly — than any other people in the world. Their personal income in 1962 reached $442.1 billion. Their tax and nontax payments to government amounted to $57.7 billion. They spent $355.4 billion on goods and services. They saved $29 billion. That is scarcely a picture of people crushed by the weight of ponderous government. Instead it suggests that a measure of security in life enlarges rather than constricts the area of personal and family freedom.

If one considers the gross national product, the picture of a strong private sector in the economy emerges even more clearly.

Gross National Product, 1962

(Billions of Dollars)

Personal Consumption Expenditures	$355.360
Gross Private Investment	78.787
Net Export of Goods and Services	3.770
Government Purchases of Goods and Services	116.977
Gross National Product	$554.894

In 1962, therefore, government spending accounted for about a fifth of the GNP — certainly not an abnormal share, especially since, as we have seen, nearly half of government outlays on goods and services went for national defense. Despite the extraordinary demands of the Cold War, which are largely responsible for the heavy tax burden, the American economy remains dominantly the creation of private enterprise.

It has been argued that if one concentrates on the trend

of government growth rather than on the size of government at the moment, the conclusion might be less reassuring. In this connection it has been pointed out that since 1952 government civilian spending has increased at a faster rate than either population or national income.

It is a fact that from 1952 to 1962 government spending on nonmilitary goods and services increased, roughly, from $30 billion to $64 billion, or about 113 percent, whereas the national income advanced only 56 percent. The vast bulk of this spending was done by state and local units of government. It went for such things as slum clearance, sewers, roads, schools, hospitals, fire and police protection. There is nothing dismaying in this. The country is still catching up on the backlog of needs that accumulated during World War II and the Korean War, as well as trying to keep abreast of population growth and the shift from cities to suburbs. If spending on public services had not increased since 1952, the country would be in deplorable shape today. Government would have failed in its duty of seeing to it that social progress keeps pace with economic growth (cf. MM, n. 168). Furthermore, despite increased government civilian spending, consumer expenditures as a percentage of GNP were as high in 1962 as at the start of the period.

If we shift the basis of our computations and include government payments under insurance programs as part of nondefense spending, the increase is greater but no more disturbing. As recently as 1956, government payments under the Old Age and Survivors Insurance Program came to only $6 billion. In 1962 they were $15.4 billion. With more and more people reaching retirement age, this is only to be expected. Somewhat similar increases have occurred in the operations of all government insurance trust funds.

The whole question of government spending can be seen in better perspective if benefit payments are considered separately from expenditures on goods and services. Far from offering any competition to consumers for goods and services, benefit payments, like interest payments on government debt, increase their demand capacity and thus strengthen private enterprise.

VI

The conclusion from this analysis is that the principle of subsidiarity cannot be used to condemn big government as it exists in the United States today. This does not imply uncritical acceptance of all government undertakings or of their size and administration. It certainly does not mean that prudent men should hold lightly Thomas Jefferson's warning that "the natural progress of things is for liberty to yield and government to gain ground." On the other hand, it does show that those who equate big government, and especially its welfare programs, with socialism, and socialism with communism, are using some other criterion than the one taught by the Popes. They are talking in the outmoded terms of economic liberalism. Their implied thesis, that no middle ground exists between laissez-faire capitalism and communism, has no support in the social teaching of the Church. Neither has the pessimistic notion that government expansion is a one-way movement that cannot be controlled, checked, or reversed by the action of free men. Pope John shows little patience with simplistic, black-and-white thinking of this kind. In *Mater et Magistra* he mentions with approval many of the activities in which governments are today engaged all over the world. He gives every indication of believing that the reformed capitalism of our times, in which the state intervenes more actively and extensively than in the past, is much closer to Christian ideals than the dog-eat-dog system that it replaced. One of the reasons is that governments are now doing a much better job of defending the rights of all classes in society and of promoting the general welfare.

CHAPTER 7

In Union There Is Strength — and Controversy

By nature men are joiners. They take to membership in groups the way ducks do to water. They come together in some geographical spot and at once set about organizing a village or a town. They like art or music and so they establish museums and symphony orchestras. They join yacht and country clubs because they enjoy golf or tennis or boating. Moved by a desire to serve the church or community, they band together to decorate altars and sanctuaries or to build playgrounds and hospitals. And so it happens, too, that men who perform the same work tend naturally and inevitably to organize around the job. They pool their resources to found corporations; they establish trade and professional associations; and they organize labor unions.

Since this tendency to associate is natural, since it flows from a social urge that God has incorporated in human beings, men have a moral right to form groupings within the larger societies of which they are members. The state may not forbid such lesser societies (except in cases where their objectives or practices are immoral or criminal), since they exist by the same title as the state itself (cf. RN, nn. 70–72).

Private societies enjoy, therefore, a certain autonomy. They are free to fix their goal, which is the private advantage of their members, and to select the means which will best enable them to reach it. Ordinarily, both the goal and the means are incorporated in a written document, which is known as the constitution or bylaws of the society. "If citizens have free right to associate," Pope Leo taught, "they also must have the right freely to adopt the organization and the rules which they judge most appropriate to achieve their purpose" (n. 76).

The autonomy of private societies is not, however, perfect or absolute. In pursuing their self-interest, they must respect the common good of the public society within which they exist and operate. So far as possible, the state should permit private societies to conduct their affairs without interference. It does have the authority, nevertheless, to intervene to pro-tect the general welfare. The price that private societies must pay, then, for their independence is social-minded and respon-sible conduct. They should have due regard both for the rights of their members and the rights of society as a whole.

From all this it follows that every human society ought to have, by divine design, an organic character. It should be composed not merely of individuals and the state, but of families and a rich multiplicity of organizations. Only in such a society can individuals grow to their full stature, helping and supporting others, and, in turn, being helped and sup-ported by them. "It is better, therefore," as we read in Scrip-ture, "that two should be together than one; for they have the advantage of their society. If one fall, he shall be sup-ported by the other. Woe to him that is alone, for when he falleth, he hath none to lift him up" (Eccl 4:9–10). And again, "A brother that is helped by his brother is like a strong city" (Prv 18:19).

I

That Pope Leo XIII had to insist on this truth for the men of his day — and that his successors have had to continue insisting on it — is one of the great tragedies of the modern age. For by the rigid logic of economic liberalism, there was no place for societies of workingmen (or, as we would say today, for labor unions) in the economic society created by the Industrial Revolution. They were widely forbidden by law on the ground that they interfered with the operation of the law of supply and demand. Specifically, they prevented wages from being determined by competition and in this way distorted production costs. They were sand in the gears of laissez-faire capitalism. Partly for this reason, and partly, too, because employers naturally want as free a hand as possible in conducting their businesses, the efforts of workers to organize in their mutual defense were almost everywhere bitterly opposed. Thus were sown the seeds of the modern class struggle. Its ugly fruits are Marxist socialism and the atmosphere of suspicion and hostility that all too often still poisons industrial relations.

In Pope Leo's judgment, the heavy responsibility of the employer class for this deplorable development was clear. He wrote in *Rerum Novarum:*

> After the old trade guilds had been destroyed in the last century, and no protection was substituted in their place, and when public institutions and legislation had cast off traditional religious teaching, it gradually came about that the present age handed over the workers, each alone and defenseless, to the inhumanity of employers and the unbridled greed of competitors. . . . The whole process of production, as well as trade in every kind of goods, has been brought almost entirely under the power of a few, so that a very few rich and exceedingly rich men have laid a yoke almost of slavery on the unnumbered masses of non-owning workers (n. 6).

Among remedies for the wretched condition of workers, Pope Leo assigned a high place to trade unions, seeing in them a modern expression of the medieval journeymen's guilds (cf. n. 69). To deny such societies the right to exist, the Pope taught, is not within the authority of the state, since the state exists to protect natural rights, not to destroy them.

In *Quadragesimo Anno*, Pope Pius XI vividly recalled Leo's defense of trade unionism:

> For at that time in many nations those at the helm of the state, plainly imbued with liberalism, were showing little favor to workers' associations; nay, rather, they openly opposed them, and while going out of their way to recognize similar organizations of other classes and show favor to them, they were with gross injustice denying the natural right to form associations to

those who needed them most to defend themselves from ill treatment at the hands of the powerful. There were even some Catholics who looked askance at the efforts of workers to form associations of this type as if they smacked of a socialistic or revolutionary spirit (n. 30).

It is interesting to note in passing that American law implicitly recognizes the natural right of workers to organize. In Title I, Section I of the National Labor Relations Act, Congress refers to "the denial of some employers of the right of employees to organize" and speaks of "protecting the exercise by workers of full freedom of association." Experience has proved, it says, "that protection by law of the right of employes to organize" results in important social and economic benefits. Plainly, in passing that law Congress was doing no more than giving legal support to a right that workers already possessed. That right could only be one of those rights called "unalienable" in the Declaration of Independence because they come from God, the Author of the natural law.

Governments were slow, however, in acknowledging this right, as Pope Pius XI said. Among the countries in the forefront of the Industrial Revolution, Belgium did not legally recognize unions until 1866, and even then only with restrictions. Germany conceded the right of free association in most industries in 1869, but did not grant full trade-union freedom until 1918. Although the British Parliament repealed the notorious Combination Acts in 1824 — which made trade unions criminal associations — British workers had to wait until 1871, when the Trade Union Act was passed, for the complete recognition of their rights. In France, the right to organize was conceded only in 1884.

The record of the United States is scarcely less deplorable. A number of factors — the fluidity of class lines compared with Europe, the individualistic spirit of a new pioneering country, apparent constitutional obstacles, and the unrelenting opposition of many employers — prevented the federal government from assuring workers the right to organize until well into the twentieth century. A partial breakthrough occurred in 1914 when Congress, by the Clayton Act, restricted the use of injunctions in labor disputes and exempted unions from suits charging restraint of trade. In 1932, the Norris-La Guardia Act further curbed the use of injunctions. It also provided that "yellow-dog" contracts could not be legally enforced. (A yellow-dog contract is one that obliges a worker, as a condition for obtaining or holding a job, to pledge that he will not join a union or participate in its affairs. It is an immoral device that American employers widely used at one time to frustrate the worker's God-given right to organize.) The first positive encouragement of unionism dates from 1926, when Congress guaranteed the right of railroad workers to free organization (Railroad Labor Disputes Act). Nine years later, in the National Labor Relations Act (Wagner Act), it extended that guarantee to all nonfarm workers engaged in interstate commerce. (Farm workers, who need the benefits of unionism more than most workers, are still deprived of legal protection of their right to organize.)

II

When *Rerum Novarum* appeared, most trade unions in Western Europe were controlled by anarchists, Marxist socialists, or other kinds of revolutionaries. Frequently linked with political parties, they pursued the goal of revolutionary change. They scorned reform through labor law and collective bargaining. Almost without exception, they were hostile to religion, regarding it as a buttress of the existing bourgeois, capitalist order. "Under these circumstances," wrote Pope Leo, "workers who are Christians must choose one of two things: either to join unions in which it is greatly to be feared that there is danger to religion, or to form their own associations. . . ." He made it clear that the second course was the one to be followed (cf. RN, n. 74).

There can be little question, then, that the unions which Pope Leo recommended were Christian unions. It would be wrong to conclude from this, however, as some in this country have done, that other types of unions are not morally acceptable. Pope Leo explained and defended the right of free association as a natural right, which means a right possessed by all men regardless of their religious belief or lack of it. Those who exercise it, therefore, for the purpose of securing for workers "an increase in the goods of body, soul and of property" (n. 76), and who pursue their goal by honest means, are acting in a thoroughly moral manner. No less than Christian unions, unions formed in this way can appeal for support to the Church's social doctrine.

Whatever doubt may have existed about Pope Leo's teaching on this point was completely resolved by his successors.

The occasion of the first clarification was a controversy in Germany over an alternative to Marxist unions. Some argued that Catholics should support the Christian unions that had sprung up in much of the country and which accepted both Catholics and Protestants as members. Others argued for strictly Catholic unions, with Protestants excluded. In response to appeals to Rome for direction, Pope St. Pius X wrote the encyclical *Singulari Quadam*, dated September 24, 1912. He said, in substance, that although Catholic unions are the ideal, interdenominational unions are not to be condemned. Catholic workers are free in conscience to join such unions. When they exercise this right, however, they should also affiliate with workingmen's organizations devoted to moral and religious education.

Although that decision settled the German controversy, it did not directly answer a companion doubt about Catholic membership in unions, variously described as secular or neutral, which profess no religion or ideology at all. Such were and are our American unions. Neither socialist nor Christian, they embrace in their ranks Catholics, Protestants, Jews, and nonbelievers. Similar unions exist in most of the English-speaking world. By analogy with the German situation, were Catholics free in conscience to join such unions?

Pope Pius XI dealt with this question in *Quadragesimo Anno*. In some countries, he said, to organize Catholic unions is inexpedient or impractical. In such circumstances, it is scarcely possible for Catholics not to join neutral unions. These unions "should always profess justice and equity and give Catholic members full freedom to care for their own conscience and obey the laws of the Church." It lies with the bishops to ascertain whether or not neutral unions fulfill these conditions, and, in the light of their findings, to grant or deny permission to join them (cf. n. 35).

Although Pope John added nothing to this teaching, he spoke of neutral unions and their Catholic members in more positive and encouraging terms than did his predecessors. After praising the work of the International Federation of Christian Trade Unions, he continued:

> We believe further that one must praise in the same way the outstanding endeavors performed in a true Christian spirit by Our beloved sons in other professional groups and workers' associations which take their inspiration from natural-law principles and show respect for freedom of conscience (MM, n. 102).

The modern American labor movement, with 18 million workers organized in the American Federation of Labor-Congress of Industrial Organizations, the Railroad Brotherhoods, the United Mine Workers, and other independent unions, is not, of course, a religious movement, any more than our political parties or our business and professional organizations are religious movements. But it is not an antireligious or even an a-religious movement either. The goals it seeks and the principles it professes are happily in accord with the moral demands of religion.

Through collective bargaining and in other ways, our unions aim at protecting the economic interests of workers and insuring them a decent standard of living. They are intent, that is, on the pursuit of justice. Equally laudable are the principles that guide them in the struggle for this goal. Years ago, by rejecting socialism, they repudiated a revolutionary solution to the social problem created by modern industrialism. Instead they defended private property. They defended free enterprise and the right of free association. They espoused a cooperative relationship between employers and workers. They defended the dignity of the individual and the rights of families. They accepted the concept of limited government. In other words, the American labor movement took its stand on principles that Catholics recognize as natural-law principles.

It is this basic moral soundness of American trade unionism, together with its traditional respect for religion, that explains the absence of a Christian labor movement in the United States. Our bishops have never deemed it necessary to discourage or forbid membership in American labor unions. They have never suggested that Catholics ought to form separate unions to preserve the purity of their faith and the integrity of their morals. On the contrary, they have on numerous occasions shown a sympathetic interest in unions; they have opposed attempts to undermine their security; they have appeared at their conventions to invoke God's blessing on them.

When Pope Pius XII established the feast of St. Joseph the Workman, and appointed that it be celebrated on May 1, our bishops asked Rome for permission to observe it instead on the first Monday of September, our Labor Day. When one stops to think of it, that petition was eloquent testimony to the soundness of the American labor movement. It meant that to American workers the first of May had no special significance. It was a Communist holiday. The unwavering anti-communism of our unions is not the least of their contributions to a just social order.

III

During the seventy years that elapsed between *Rerum Novarum* and *Mater et Magistra*, sweeping changes occurred in the capitalistic system. Karl Marx's prediction of a future of deepening misery for workers proved to be false. Even by the time *Quadragesimo Anno* appeared, signs of improvement in their lot were clear and striking. Compared with Leo's times, Pope Pius XI observed with satisfaction, "The condition of workers has been improved and made more equitable"; in the most advanced and wealthy countries "the workers can no longer be considered universally overwhelmed with misery and lacking the necessities of life" (QA, n. 59).

Since World War II, progress has been even more striking. Protected by law, trade unions have spread almost everywhere. In the developed countries they are, with scarcely any exception, one of the most powerful forces in society. Like all other social institutions, they have undergone changes as they struggled to cope with new situations and challenges. Pope John refers to this when he notes in Mater et Magistra that unions "no longer unite workers for the sake of conflict, but rather for joint effort — principally in the field of collective bargaining" (n. 97). He is describing here, of course, the promising evolution of some European unions from dogmatic Marxism to a more pragmatic, less class-conscious approach to life.

Pope John notes, also, that further change impends.

"We cannot fail to emphasize," he says, "how imperative or at least highly opportune it is that workers should be able freely to make their voices heard and listened to beyond the confines of their individual productive units and at every level of society." The reason is obvious. In our highly organized modern economies, it frequently happens that the most important decisions are not those made by individual companies but "those made by public authorities, or by institutions that function on a world-wide or national scale." One has only to think of the international commodity agreements that have been negotiated since the war, or of the General Agreement on Tariffs and Trade (GATT), or of the Iron and Steel Community in Western Europe to realize the truth of the Holy Father's observations. Furthermore, almost all European countries are engaged in national economic planning of some kind, so that the decisions of the planners have a greater impact on wages, prices, and production goals than do the decisions of company managements. It is "appropriate and necessary" in these circumstances, says the Pope, that workers, as well as capitalists, should have a voice on these higher levels of decision-making (cf. nn. 98–99).

In the United States, we have nothing that resembles the economic planning institutions of Western Europe. The nearest approach — and it is a very remote one — is the Advisory Council on Labor-Management Policy which President John F. Kennedy established to assist the government in formulating programs in the industrial field. Organized labor, as well as industry and the public, is represented on the council.

Labor's voice in matters that concern workers — and in nonlabor matters as well — is heard in other ways in this country. Union representatives testify on a wide variety of bills that come before Congress and state legislatures. They are able to make their views known to the executive agencies that administer labor and welfare legislation. They serve on temporary commissions which the President sets up from time to time to study great public issues. They have been actively involved in the foreign-aid program, going back as far as the Marshall Plan. As for government decisions that affect entire industries and even the whole economy — decisions on tariff levels, on taxes and public spending, and on monetary policy — labor is as free to talk as any other group in our society. Ultimately, however, the sole responsibility for decisions of this kind rests with government. If the time ever comes when private groups are asked to assume a more active role in formulating public programs and in administering them, unions will certainly be as prominently involved as the owners of capital.

Pope John's reference to the inadequacy of collective bargaining may recall to Americans some fairly fresh pages of labor history. After the founding of the American Federation of Labor in the nineteenth century, trade unions relied almost exclusively on collective bargaining to achieve their objectives. They were suspicious of government, of legislatures as well as courts, and they hoped for no more from federal and state authorities than neutrality in industrial disputes and freedom from interference in carrying on union activities. Although they were never completely indifferent to politics, their participation in elections was secondary and subordinate to the job of organizing the unorganized and winning fair contracts from employers. This reliance on their own united strength was known as voluntarism.

Only gradually did unquestioning faith in voluntarism die; it took a generation or more before unions came to see that they could never achieve their goals for workers without government help. Indeed, the full realization did not dawn until the 1930's, and then it came only as a by-product of the despair caused by the great depression. While it remains true that unions still place their main reliance on collective bargaining, they have over the past quarter century vastly enlarged their political activities. It is chiefly in this way that they exert a rightful influence on those public agencies whose decisions are so important for social progress and economic advance. There can be no question, then, of the moral right of unions to organize for political education and action, although this course is not, unfortunately, without dangers.

IV

In defending the right of workers to organize, Pope Leo and his successors thought of unions as defenders of the rights of their members, not as instruments of class warfare. The Popes denied that hatred is inherent in the employer-employee relationship. "Each needs the other completely," wrote Pope Leo, "neither capital can do without labor, nor labor without capital" (RN, n. 28). Furthermore, the Pope reminded us, workers and employers are alike sons of God. They have been redeemed by the blood of Christ. They are brothers. Aware that each has rights which the other is bound to respect, that each has duties which he is bound to discharge, they could find in Christian teaching a bond not merely of friendship but even of brotherly love (cf. nn. 29–33).

Clearly, the Popes hoped that by eliminating a justified grievance of workers — the denial by employers of their right to organize and the refusal to bargain collectively with them — they were laying the foundation for a more equitable and peaceful relationship.

The Popes were aware, naturally, that there are elements of discord in the employer-employee relationship. To mention one, the possibility of disagreement always exists over distribution of the fruits of their common effort. What share should go to workers in wages? What to owners in dividends? What to management in salaries and bonuses? What share should be retained in the business for modernization and expansion of facilities? To mention another source of discord, one which in recent years has bedeviled industrial relations, what emphasis should be placed on technological progress and productive efficiency, and what stress on job security? If management installs a new machine that displaces a score of workers, what provision, if any, should be made for them? Should they be given generous separation allowances? Should they be retrained and offered other jobs in the company? Should they be helped financially to move their families to other communities? Or should they simply be fired?

Despite these and other conflicts of interest, the Popes believe that what employers and workers have in common is so self-evident and tangible that it furnishes a solid foundation for a friendly, cooperative relationship. On a purely selfish, material basis, they have a strong mutual interest in the success of the enterprise. If the business fails to operate profitably, if it cannot produce a good or service at a price the public is willing to pay, it is of no value whatsoever to either the owners or the workers.

On a higher plane, employers and workers have in common, or should have in common, the desire to serve their fellowmen and to make some contribution to the happiness and prosperity of society. In this way they dedicate the work of their hands and minds to God, and use their property as faithful stewards of the Master.

To give this community of interest concrete expression, Pope Pius XI suggested in *Quadragesimo Anno* that besides unions and trade associations workers and employers should establish joint councils of some kind that would enable them to come together, not as buyers and sellers of labor, but as partners in production (cf. nn. 83–87). The idea has been much discussed both here and abroad, but in this country, at least, little has come of it.

Why has not more progress been made along these lines? Why have not the Church's hopes for collective bargaining been more fully realized? Why is management literature so consistently critical of unions, and union literature so hostile to management? Why are employers and unions so far apart on many public issues? Why do so many employers continue to oppose, not only joint labor-management programs, but even the efforts of workers to organize and bargain collectively? Why is there more concern with the letter of the law in industrial relations than with the common good?

The answer to these questions is very complex. It must take into account the sad legacy of the past, since memories of injustice remain vivid for many years after the event. It must allow for attitudes and practices in the business community that still reflect the influence of economic liberalism. It must note a native individualism that disposes many Americans to look on unionism with a jaundiced eye. Above all, it must include some consideration of the weakness of human nature and the perennial difficulty of subjecting economic activities to the yoke of morality. This should not be surprising. In all walks of life, we are constantly reminded of the gap between our ethical ideals and our daily practice. Life will always be a struggle, and at some time or other all men must humbly confess with St. Paul: "For I do not that which I will; but the

evil which I hate, that I do" (Rom 7:15). The battle for good
relations between labor and management, like the fight for good
social relations generally, will never be fully won.

During the postwar period, the public has been shocked
from time to time by scandals in both labor and industry.
In the late 1950's, protracted hearings before the Senate Select
Committee on Improper Activities in the Labor or Management Field (McClellan Committee) revealed before a nationwide television audience a sordid story of financial irregularities
and denial of democratic rights in a number of unions. Also
spread on the record were shady practices of some otherwise
respectable corporations. As a result of the Senate investigation,
Congress passed the Landrum-Griffin Act — a law that makes it
more difficult for racketeers and dishonest labor leaders to exploit the rank and file, and curbs the license of employers to
finance underhanded antiunion activities. Meanwhile organized
labor, through the adoption by the AFL-CIO of codes of ethical
practice, has made efforts to clean its own house, and a number of employers have shown new interest in creating a better
moral climate in industry.

Long ago, Pope Leo insisted that no satisfactory solution
of the problems of industrial relations could be found apart
from religion and morality (cf. RN, n. 24). Our American
experience amply confirms that judgment.

V

Yet it is easy to exaggerate the gloomy side of industrial
relations, especially if one occupies a comfortable seat on the
sidelines and has never experienced the heat of conflict on
the field. The communications media — press, radio, and television — contribute to, if they do not often create, a distorted
view of the proceedings. It is notorious that strife is judged
to be more newsworthy than peaceful progress. It comes as a
surprise to many newspaper readers to discover that thousands
of labor-management agreements are negotiated every year

without fuss or fanfare, and that time lost through industrial disputes is only a tiny fraction of total hours worked. In 1962, the public was fed a heavy diet of black headlines telling of a construction strike on the Pacific Coast, a longshore strike on the East and Gulf Coasts, newspaper strikes in Cleveland and New York, and a transportation strike in Philadelphia. It was not told subsequently, certainly not in headlines, that in all of 1962 time lost through strikes amounted approximately to $16/100$ of 1 percent of man-days worked.

Furthermore, many people have no idea of the tedious, grubby work that goes on day after day, in stores, factories, and mines all over the country, to build a kind of common law of industrial life. It is not widely enough realized that the happiness and satisfaction of workers are frequently more closely bound up with conditions surrounding the job than they are with the compensation received for it. Men want above all to be treated as men. They want their rights respected. They don't want to live at the whim of a boss, no matter how fair and considerate he may happen to be. They want some say in the decisions that affect them.

To the satisfaction of these human needs and demands, collective bargaining makes a precious contribution; and it does so, for the most part, without strikes or other interruptions of work. It is a rare labor-management contract nowadays that does not provide for the peaceful resolution of all disputes arising under it. The growth of grievance procedure in American industry, culminating in voluntary but binding arbitration, is one of the great moral achievements of our times.

This entire development is completely in accord with Catholic social doctrine. In *Mater et Magistra*, Pope John emphasized that there is more to justice than a fair distribution of wealth and income:

> Justice is to be observed not only in the distribution of wealth resulting from production, but also with respect to the conditions under which production takes place. For there is an

innate demand in human nature that when men engage in production they should have the opportunity of exercising responsibility and of perfecting their personalities.

It follows that if the organization and operation of an
economic system are such as to compromise the human dignity
of those who engage in it, or to blunt their sense of responsibility, or to impede the exercise of personal initiative, such an
economic system is unjust. And this is so even if, by hypothesis,
the wealth produced through such a system reaches a high level
and this wealth is distributed according to standards of justice
and equity (nn. 82–83).

A little further on in the encyclical, the Pope explains how
natural it is for workers to desire some voice in the enterprise
in which they are employed. They are not to be treated as
"mere silent performers who have no chance to bring their
experience into play." True, there must be authority and unity
of direction if the business is to produce efficiently, but the
rights of management can and must be reconciled with an
active role for workers. The way to a solution lies in giving
to industrial enterprises "the characteristics of a true human
community," where "relations between employers and directors
on the one hand, and employes on the other, [are] marked by
respect, appreciation, understanding, loyal and active co-opera-
tion, and devotion to their common undertaking." In such an
enterprise, work will be regarded and performed, "not merely
as a source of income, but also as the fulfillment of a duty
and the performance of a service to others" (nn. 91–93).

Enlightened managements are aware of the need, and sometimes of the duty, to treat workers as individuals, not just as
names on the payroll. More and more it is coming to be
accepted as axiomatic that good industrial relations are good
human relations. Over the past quarter century an extensive
"human-relations" literature has been developed, and terms
like "participation" and "two-way communications" are now
part of the managerial vocabulary. On more than one occasion,
Pope Pius XII referred approvingly to this development, noting
that the behavioral sciences, far from finding any conflict be-

tween religious ideals and profitable industrial relations, had confirmed a constructive connection between them (cf. address to Directors of Chemical Products Organizations, January 10, 1958). It is possible, though, that managements which adopt a human-relations program merely because it is good business may be disappointed in the results. Though techniques are important — more important than those in authority sometimes realize — they are no substitute for the respect and affection that are the soul of all good human relations. No better rule for employer-employee relationships was ever given than the teaching of Christ that whatever we do to the least of His brothers, we do to Him (cf. Mt 25:40).

VI

Despite intelligence and goodwill on both sides, however, disputes between employers and unions are as inevitable as quarrels between wives and husbands. In a system of free enterprise, the right of workers to strike and the right of employers to lock out their employees are inseparable from collective bargaining. The alternative is compulsory arbitration not only of disputes arising under an existing contract ("disputes of rights") but also of disputes over the terms of a new contract ("disputes of interests"). Since in practice compulsory arbitration of disputes of interests means government dictation of the terms of employment, almost all democracies have rejected it. In this country, employers and unions, even those which accept binding arbitration of disputes of rights, are equally opposed to it. So are knowledgeable people generally. They appreciate that the corollary of government wage-fixing is government price-fixing. Although nobody questions the need for limited government regulation of prices, as in the case of public utilities that are natural monopolies, everybody recognizes that the extension of price regulation to all industry would lead to a state-planned economy. Because democratic peoples set such high value on liberty, they prefer the risks and costs of occasional industrial conflict to the suffocating security of a lockstep economy.

On the other hand, no democracy leaves unions and employers completely free to settle their differences as they see fit. The practice of picketing is regulated, and all resort to violence is outlawed. Furthermore, before strikes can be legally called, the parties must accept the services of public mediators in an effort to reach agreement. In cases where a dispute threatens the health or safety of the community, procedures are established, as in the Railroad Labor Disputes Act and the Taft-Hartley Act, which have the effect of postponing a strike until all peaceful means of settling the dispute have been exhausted.

Legislation of this kind is reasonable and necessary. It is a price that employers and unions should willingly pay to preserve free collective bargaining. So long as it is fair to both parties, it tends to reinforce the four classical conditions of a just strike that bind unions independently of any human law. (Substantially the same conditions bind employers in their use of the lockout.)

The first of these is a just cause, such as the refusal of an employer to pay fair wages, or to recognize the union and bargain collectively.

The second is a reasonable hope of success. It is obviously unjust to ask workers to undergo the severe privations of a strike for an unattainable objective. It does not follow from this, however, that a lost strike is always in vain.

The third is proportion between the gains hoped for and the suffering caused by the strike. When the entire community is affected, the decision to strike places an exceptionally heavy onus on the unions. The community must be willing, however, to accept some inconvenience; otherwise it would be indifferent to injustice and lacking in charity.

The fourth is the duty to exhaust all peaceful procedures before resorting to the ultimate weapon of the strike.

To apply these moral criteria with some degree of certitude

is no easy or simple task. It is often impossible for those not engaged in the negotiations to know what the real issues are. Even when these are known, only those familiar with the industry have the necessary background for an informed judgment. Since in the nature of things unions are usually cast in the role of aggressors — they make *demands* on the employer — one must guard against a tendency to blame them for all breakdowns in negotiations. If a strike is called because an employer refuses to concede just demands, the responsibility for it rests on him and not on the union. In effect, by giving the union no alternative except to submit to injustice and betray the interests of its members, he forces the strike.

Just as peace among nations remains an ideal toward which all God-fearing men must strive, so, too, labor-management peace. But the peace aimed at is not peace at any price. It does not consist in the mere absence of conflict, much less in a cozy relationship that exploits the public. It is, in St. Augustine's phrase, "the work of justice." That is why Pope Leo exhorted governments, not to outlaw strikes, but to remove the injustices that cause them (cf. RN, n. 56). Those who are impatient with industrial discord and want a law against it might occasionally remind themselves that there are no strikes behind the Iron and Bamboo Curtains.

CHAPTER 8

Problems of Industrial Relations

The basic considerations underlying a moral approach to the socioeconomic order are, as the reader has probably concluded by now, relatively few in number. They include the nature of man and the end of human life; the purpose of natural resources and the means of developing them; the role of private ownership and the function of public authority; the area of individual action and the place of group effort; the nature of work and its remuneration; the roles of justice and charity as directive norms for individual and organized activity.

Once the task of determining what the revelation of Christ and the natural law require in all these matters has been done, it does not have to be done all over again. When the principles have been established, they have been established for all time.

This does not mean that the Church's social teaching is static. First of all, the principles themselves are capable of refinement and development. Second, the principles must be freshly adapted to the changes that are always in progress in economic society. Explaining the need for a new encyclical forty years after *Rerum Novarum*, Pope Pius XI referred to these dynamic elements in the Church's social doctrine:

> Yet in the course of these same years certain doubts have arisen concerning either the correct meaning of some parts of Leo's encyclical or conclusions to be deduced therefrom. . . . Furthermore, since new needs and changed conditions of our age have made necessary a more precise application of Leo's teaching or even additions thereto, We most gladly seize this fitting occasion . . . to answer, so far as in Us lies, these doubts and demands of the present day (QA, n. 40).

In the same encyclical Pope Pius distinguished between the Church's social doctrine and "Catholic social science." The science was developed by Catholic scholars and writers who studied the doctrine and applied it in different places and circumstances (cf. nn. 19–20). In the years following World War II, this process of application has been stimulated in the United States by a number of developments that have had a notable impact on trade unionism and collective bargaining. We shall consider some of the more important ones here, beginning with the still smoldering controversy over so-called "right-to-work" laws.

I

The right-to-work movement is a peculiarly American phenomenon which, in its present form, dates from a Florida law adopted in 1944. By stipulating that "the right of persons to work shall not be denied or abridged on account of membership or nonmembership in any labor union," that law banned all the usual types of union security — chiefly the closed shop, the union shop, and maintenance of membership. Thus the movement is a continuation, under a new, appealing, but deceptive formula, of the open-shop drive that reactionary forces in United States industry mounted in the early years of the century. For this reason, despite protestations to the contrary — some of which are sincere — it has strong antiunion overtones. It has done more, perhaps, than anything else in the postwar period to embitter industrial relations in the United States.

It should be clearly understood that the right-to-work controversy has nothing to do with an old European quarrel over the right to work. Socialists formerly contended that an unemployed man had a right to demand a job of the state, and the state had a duty to provide him with one. Catholics replied (1) that since man has a duty to work, he certainly has a right to work, but (2) that this does not mean that the state is obliged to give every man a job. What it does mean is that the state must use its resources to promote prosperity and prevent unemployment, and that it must see to it, through social insurance or other means, that the jobless, during periods of unemployment, have a subsistence income.

In another respect, too, the right-to-work controversy over here has no counterpart in European continental experience. From the beginning, modern European unionism was a weapon in the hands of revolutionaries — who were Marxists more often than not — to overthrow existing economic, political, and religious institutions. There was an element of conspiracy about it. Sometimes the real leaders of the movement — the men who issued orders — were unknown. In every case, they ambitioned a monopoly control of jobs, so that the full power of the proletariat would be at their disposal.

That is the unionism which Pope Leo had in mind when he described unions "largely under the control of secret leaders . . . who apply principles which are in harmony with neither Christianity nor the welfare of states," and who, having gained control over job opportunities, "contrive that those who refuse to join with them will be forced by want to pay the penalty" (RN, n. 74). That also appears to be the kind of unionism which Pope Pius XII was thinking of when he wondered skeptically how the personal rights of workers could be protected "by an anonymous group, working through the agency of immense organizations which are of their very nature monopolies" (Christmas Message, 1952).

Admittedly, there is some obscurity about that passage from the 1952 Christmas Message, but almost all American commentators agree that it has little, if any, reference to unionism in the United States. Although American unions are in a sense monopolies — under our labor laws a union that has bargaining rights in a company is legally empowered and obliged to represent all workers in the bargaining unit whether they are union members or not — they are by no stretch of the imagination anonymous. On the contrary, they are well known, and so are their leaders. In our American experience, only in communist-dominated unions do labor leaders take orders from an anonymous source, namely, the communist party.

It is not possible, then, to settle the right-to-work dispute by appealing to papal documents. Nowhere do they mention it. Similarly, one will look in vain through the annual statements of the American hierarchy for any reference to the controversy. About a dozen bishops, however, have made important pronouncements on it, as we shall see. Before noting some of these, let us first try to understand more precisely what the quarrel is all about.

From the beginning of labor organization in the United States, going back even to colonial times, union members tried to prevent competition among workers for jobs. They did this to protect their wages and working conditions from the uncontrolled operation of the law of supply and demand. The means normally used was to refuse to work side by side with nonunion men, who were willing to accept inferior terms of employment. Typical of union practice was the following provision from the constitution of the Baltimore Typographical Society, adopted in 1842:

> Every person working at the business will be required to make application to join this Society within one month from the time of his commencing work at any office in the city. . . . On the refusal or neglect to comply with these regulations . . . the members of this Society will cease to work in any office where such person may be employed.

As a result of this union practice, two institutional arrangements, known as the closed shop and the union shop, took deep root in a number of industries — printing, construction, cigar making, carpet weaving, hat making. The closed shop is an arrangement, agreed to by an employer and a union, that obliges the company to hire and employ only union members. The union shop is the same arrangement with the difference that the employer is free to hire nonunion men. As a condition for continued employment, however, the new employees must become and remain members of the union.

Two variations of these arrangements, which represent a compromise between union demands for a closed or union shop and employer refusal to grant them, came into wide acceptance during World War II and the years following. The first, called maintenance of membership, requires all workers who are union members to remain members during the life of a collective-bargaining agreement. The second, known as the agency shop, obliges nonunion workers to pay the equivalent of dues to a union in return for its services as bargaining agent.

In many cases where one or the other of these types of union security is in force, employers agree to "check off" dues and pay them directly to the union.

The passage of the Taft-Hartley Act in 1947 made substantial changes in union-security arrangements. The law prohibited the closed shop, as well as all union-conducted hiring halls that provide employers with only union members. It permitted the union shop, but under such severe limitations as to change radically its character. Employers and unions were permitted (not obliged) to agree to a union shop only if a majority of the employees, in a secret, government-sponsored election, authorized the union to negotiate it. Employers were forbidden to discharge a worker who failed to join the union or maintain membership in it for any reason other than "the failure of the employee to tender the periodic dues and the initiation fees uniformly required as a condition of acquiring or retaining union membership." Thus unions could still expel members for cause, but they lost the power in such cases to deprive the worker of his job. As additional protection for the individual worker, the law stipulated that unions would commit an unfair labor practice if they charged dues and assessments which the National Labor Relations Board found "excessive or discriminatory under all the circumstances." (In 1959, the Landrum-Griffith Act expanded the legal protections of the rights of union members.)

Finally, the Taft-Hartley Act provided that workers who

authorized a union shop could, if 30 percent of their number so requested, seek an NLRB election to terminate the union shop. A majority vote against the union shop would oblige the employer to cease requiring union membership as a condition of employment.

If the Taft-Hartley Act had stopped there, the right-to-work controversy might never have arisen. However, the law went on to provide, in Section 14 (b), that nothing in the act should be construed as permitting union-shop agreements "in any State or Territory in which such execution or application is prohibited by State or Territorial law." By this abdication of authority over union-security arrangements in interstate commerce, Congress opened the way to the right-to-work movement. Within a matter of months, ten states, all of them in the South, where antiunion sentiment is strong, and the agricultural Midwest outlawed the union shop and other types of union security. In the autumn of 1963, twenty states had right-to-work laws. Only one of these, Indiana, could be considered an industrial state.

Meanwhile, the original union-shop provisions of the Taft-Hartley Act have been changed in one important and illuminating respect. In 1951, heeding requests from embarrassed employers as well as others, Congress repealed the clause requiring a majority vote of the employees as a condition for negotiating a union-shop contract. By that time it had become clear that the basic assumption justifying the election procedure — that the workers themselves did not want the union shop and needed protection against dictatorial union leaders — was completely false. In 46,119 elections conducted by the NLRB between August, 1947, and October, 1951, more than 5½ million votes were cast for the union shop. That was 91 percent of all votes cast. In 97.1 percent of the elections the workers authorized the union shop.

These overwhelming majorities provided convincing proof of what many students of the labor movement had long suspected, namely, that the vast majority of American blue-collar workers prefer to work under union-shop conditions. (In 1946, prior to the Taft-Hartley Act, 11 million of approximately 15 million workers covered by collective-bargaining agreements enjoyed some form of union security — 3.7 million had maintenance of membership; 3.4 million, the closed shop; and 4 million, the union shop.) Far from justifying the opposition of many employers to the union shop, the elections put pressure on them to grant it. So the election provision of the Taft-Hartley Act boomeranged.

The failure of the election approach to stop union-shop agreements stimulated employer interest in right-to-work laws. Numerous and well-financed efforts were made in many states to pass such laws, and in nine cases since 1951 these were successful. They failed, however, in such large industrial states as Ohio and California. This is understandable because not all employers by any means sympathize with or support the right-to-work movement. They have learned from experience that the union shop can make a valuable contribution to good industrial relations.

Catholic social scientists have been keenly interested in the union-security controversy because the arguments on both sides lean heavily on moral principles.

Opponents of the union shop contend that it violates the right of individuals to work, without paying dues to a union, for any employer who will hire them. Only public societies, they say, have the right to compel membership and impose taxes. They also argue that since unions are infected by materialism and are guilty of corrupt practices, it is unjust to force workers to belong to them as a condition for obtaining and holding a job.

Trade unions insist that workers who refuse to join the union that is legally obliged to represent their interests are selfish and irresponsible. They reap where others have sown; they have no sense of obligation to their fellow workers. Unions also say that without the security of the union shop it is difficult for them to control irresponsible members and act constructively in their relations with employers. They point out, finally, that in industries where employment is intermittent or casual, as in the building trades and longshoring, unions cannot exist without the union shop.

Weighing these arguments against an American background, most Catholic social scientists who have written about the dispute oppose right-to-work laws and defend the union shop.

As they see it, the crux of the controversy is the nature of the right to work. This right is clearly not a claim to a specific job, but rather a general right corresponding to the duty incumbent on all men to work to support themselves. In practice, this right depends for its exercise on the willingness of an employer to provide a job. It is hedged about by other conditions as well. The employer may stipulate that the worker report at a certain time, that he remain on the job until a whistle blows signaling the end of the shift, that he perform the work assigned as directed by a foreman, that he observe safety rules, that he not smoke, that he agree to deductions of social-security taxes from his pay, that he dress in a certain way, that he observe other regulations that are necessary for the orderly and efficient conduct of the plant community.

So the right to work is not an absolute right nor a purely individualistic one. Both the employer and the government can and do limit its exercise in numerous ways.

The key question then becomes: May a majority of workers banded together in a union also impose conditions on the individual's right to work?

Only a brief consideration is necessary to show that unions do in fact determine many of the conditions that surround jobs in this country. They do so legally, since the Taft-Hartley Act not only permits but, as we have seen, obliges the union representing a majority of the employees to bargain for all the employees. Thus the terms of the collective-bargaining agreement govern all the jobs in the plant. The acceptance of these arrangements is as much a condition of the employee's right to work as are the conditions imposed by the employer. Whoever accepts collective bargaining in the American environment must, therefore, logically concede the moral right of unions to exercise this power over jobs.

But does this power include the right to insist on union membership as a condition of employment?

Before answering that question, it is helpful to recall what the union shop is. As was explained above, under the Taft-Hartley Act it is little more than a device for compelling all the members of a bargaining unit to give financial support to the bargaining agent. Only in the case where the union expels a member for failure to pay dues may it demand that the employer discharge the worker for nonmembership in the union. In the concrete, therefore, the question is this: May the union require all those in the bargaining unit to pay their fair share of the costs of representing them?

The vast majority of Catholic social scientists answer in the affirmative. It seems to them that in the circumstances the union's demand is reasonable. It does no violence to any right of the employee. On the contrary, the employee appears to have a duty of some kind, arising from charity toward his fellow workers, if not from justice, to support the union apart from any external compulsion.

This last consideration raises the larger question of the duty of workers to join unions. All Catholic authorities agree that workers are under a general obligation to join unions, in the same way that men are under a general obligation to marry and propagate the race. But just as some men are free not to marry, so some workers, according to one school of thought, are free not to join unions. So long as enough workers organize to make unionism an effective force for justice in economic society, individuals are relieved of a specific duty to join a union. Those who hold this doctrine concede, however, that where membership is necessary for the survival of a union, or for its honest and effective operation, workers have a duty to join.

Another school of thought maintains that in modern industrial society every worker is morally obliged to join a union. In a pastoral letter in February, 1950, the hierarchy of Quebec argued the case in this way:

> Every man has an obligation to seek to protect the security of his professional interests. He has the duty to seek to obtain for himself and his family all that is necessary in order to live a truly human life and to safeguard them against future hazards. He has the duty to contribute to the welfare of his fellows, especially those united to him in common interests. He has the duty to collaborate in restoring a social order which would be more balanced in favoring respect for justice in all the activities of labor, industry and commerce. The isolated worker cannot do this. But union with his fellow workers will permit him to fulfill this imperious social duty. In the present state of things, accordingly, there exists a moral obligation to participate actively in one's economic organization.

That argument assumes, naturally, as does the argument against right-to-work laws, that there is question of legitimate unions, unions which, at a minimum, are based on natural-law principles and respect the religious beliefs of their members. There is no obligation, obviously, to join a union dominated by racketeers or communists, or one that practices racial or religious discrimination.

To return to the union-shop problem. As was said earlier, some supporters of right-to-work laws make the point that only the public society has the powers of compulsion and taxation. By obliging workers to become members and pay dues, unions are said to claim an authority that no private society has.

This argument assumes that unions are purely private societies, like the Knights of Columbus or the Benevolent and Protective Order of Elks. Although it is true that a few old-fashioned labor leaders still think of them in these terms, unions today are "affected by a public interest." They perform quasi-public functions. While they are not instruments of the government, as in the Soviet Union, they are authorized by law to represent workers in collective bargaining. Furthermore, not only must they follow in their relationships with employers procedures laid down by the government; they are also obliged to bring their internal administration into conformity with publicly established standards. They are, in short, private societies, but of a special kind. In this respect, they may be likened to bar associations and medical societies, which, though private, exercise as much control over lawyers and doctors as unions do over workers. In many states, bar associations and medical societies have the equivalent of a closed shop.

Without private societies of this kind, exercising considerable powers of self-government under the general supervision of the state, the ideal of an organic society cannot be realized. It is strange that those who have in their cultural inheritance the rich experience of the medieval guilds do not understand this. One can only surmise that the spirit of economic liberalism, with its highly individualistic concept of human rights, still exerts considerable influence in modern society.

Another argument of right-to-work proponents, that American unions are a danger to the morals of workers because they are infected by materialism, has failed to persuade most Catholic authorities. There is no evidence that trade unions are any more materialistic than is American society as a whole. If they were dangerously materialistic, or extensively corrupt, our bishops would be obliged to condemn them and warn Catholics against participating in their affairs. They have not done so. Instead, on a number of occasions, individual bishops, far from being stampeded by charges of materialism and corruption, have publicly opposed the drive to outlaw the union shop. Not that these bishops are indifferent to such abuses as exist in unions. They are not. They insist, however, that the sensible course is to attack abuses directly, rather than to eliminate them by the socially destructive tactic of destroying the good institutions in which they may inhere.

In the course of legislative hearings in the spring of 1957 on a proposed right-to-work law in Connecticut, Archbishop

Henry J. O'Brien of Hartford issued a statement flatly denying the basic moral argument for the law:

The sponsors of the proposed legislation claim that the fundamental right of the individual is invaded if he must join a union. I do not agree with this viewpoint. It is neither immoral nor unethical to require union membership for the greater common good of the group. In our modern and complex society, everyone is subject to prohibitions and restraints, as well as to mandatory rules of conduct based on the common good of the group.

The following year the bishops of Ohio joined in approving a statement opposing a right-to-work bill in that state:

Man has a right and duty to work for his livelihood. This right cannot be circumscribed to the extent that a man loses his liberty of choice or a vocation; nor to the extent that he is deprived of an opportunity to support himself and his family. It does not follow that a man has the unconditional right to work in any and every industry or business at will.

For reasons of social justice it may be desirable and often advantageous to the common good that man's right be restricted by certain specified conditions. One of these imposed conditions may require that he belong to a labor union or at least be obliged to join the union subsequently, so as to share responsibility with his fellow workmen in support of the union. . . .

If state statutes were to make such a condition of union maintenance mandatory, we would oppose them as unwise, if not unjust. If state statutes however were to forbid the enforcement of such a condition, when mutually accepted by management and labor through collective bargaining, then we would be equally opposed.

Earlier Archbishop Joseph F. Rummel of New Orleans, personally and through an official spokesman, had opposed a right-to-work bill in Louisiana. Besides insisting that the right to work is not purely individualistic and absolute, the Archbishop, in a telegram to the State Senate Industrial Relations Committee, June 1, 1954, attacked the bill on other grounds:

It is a misnomer because it actually denies what it pretends to give, namely, the right to work.

It is reactionary because it nullifies all that has been accomplished in our State through the organized labor movement for the mutual benefit of working classes and the stability of industry.

It is insincere because, while it pretends to guarantee the right to work, it actually frustrates that right, in effect exposing labor to lose security, a decent standard of living and humane working conditions. It makes a mockery of the constitutional right to organize for the common good and welfare. It invites continuing and recurring social strife and discontent. In a word, it is unfair and unsocial class legislation contrary to the common good.

In a letter to the New York *Labor Leader*, in April, 1955, Archbishop Robert E. Lucey of San Antonio was even more caustic. "The efforts of certain evil interests to foist the fraudulent 'right-to-work' law on the people of several States," he said, "is a sad commentary on their greed, selfishness and stupidity."

Such statements may seem somewhat harsh, but they reflect the judgment of most Catholic social scientists that the right-to-work movement is aimed, not at protecting the rights of individual workers, but at weakening unions and undermining collective bargaining. This is a serious matter to men who regard collective bargaining as essential to social justice and the safeguarding of the dignity of the individual worker. Furthermore, Catholic social thinkers, who see no practical alternative to Marxist class struggle except collective bargaining, are fearful of the effects of the right-to-work drive on labor-management relations. Already it is apparent to them that this drive, reflecting as it does a thinly veiled hostility to organized labor, has aroused a strong class feeling in many union circles.

Finally, Catholic social leaders cannot help noticing that the right-to-work movement is powered almost exclusively by employers and extremists on the far right. This naturally engenders some suspicion about the motives of the movement's sponsors, especially since the workers themselves don't seem to feel in most cases that the union shop violates their right to work. On the contrary, they are firmly persuaded that the best guarantee of their right to work — for fair wages and in decent surroundings — is a strong and secure trade union. To the vast majority of union members the union shop appears not as a restrictive or tyrannizing force but as a liberating one.

II

Right-to-work laws are not the only cloud over unionism and collective bargaining today.

There is, for example, the growing pressure on government to intervene in collective bargaining, a pressure resulting from circumstances that are likely to be with us for a long time.

The first circumstance is the rapid pace of technological change. This is creating problems of job erosion and worker displacement that are severely taxing the capacity of even well-meaning employers and unions to solve.

The second is the growing strain of the Cold War. For a number of years now the United States has had a big deficit in its international payments. We have been spending and lending abroad much more than foreigners have been spending and lending here. Since foreigners are free to demand gold for their surplus dollars, our gold supply has sharply declined. At some point or other, this process must be stopped to preserve the integrity of the dollar.

There are basically two ways to stop it. One is to cut back drastically on our foreign economic and military commitments. That would mean recalling troops from South Korea, West Germany, and other places, stopping military and defense-support aid to our allies, and cutting the underdeveloped countries loose to shift for themselves. The second way is to increase our foreign-trade surplus, that is, to widen the already sizable margin by which our exports exceed our imports.

Since the Johnson administration does not want to weaken the free world and risk losing the Cold War, any more than the Eisenhower and Kennedy administrations did, it has followed its predecessors in choosing the second alternative. As a consequence, it is intensely interested in keeping American goods competitive in foreign markets. It is very much concerned, therefore, with wage and price movements in the private sector of the economy.

During the latter years of the Eisenhower administration, the government showed this concern by repeated exhortations to labor and management to exercise economic statesmanship. By this is meant that unions and employers should not make wage agreements that forced price increases, since price increases conflicted with the government's economic objectives.

Under President Kennedy, government exhortations became both more specific and more vigorous. Management and labor negotiators were put under pressure to follow "guidelines" in wage bargaining. Although the guidelines, which aimed at keeping wage increases within the average annual increase in productivity, did not have the rigidity of a yardstick, they were sufficiently restrictive to modify traditional approaches to collective bargaining. This was especially true when insistence on guidelines was coupled with government demands for strike-free settlements.

Still a third factor encouraging government intervention is the concentration of massive economic power in both unions and corporations. This challenges one of the assumptions that underlay the government's encouragement of collective bargaining in the 1930's.

During the debate on the Wagner Bill, guaranteeing the right of workers to organize, Senator David I. Walsh explained that the objective was to escort the chosen agents of the employees "to the door of the employer and say, 'Here they are, the legal representatives of your employees.' What happens behind those doors is not inquired into, and the bill does not seek to inquire into it." Although the Senator from Massachusetts was chiefly intent on reassuring opponents of the bill that its purpose was to impose on employers an obligation to bargain in good faith, not an obligation to accede to the union's demands, his remarks had a wider significance. They carried the implication that so far as the economic substance of the collective-bargaining agreement went, government could safely follow a hands-off policy. It could do so on the premise that competition would force both parties to be reasonable.

Since that assumption was deemed basic to an economic system ruled by supply and demand in a free market, since it was clearly in the tradition of American capitalism, no one bothered at the time to question it. Even though by the mid-1930's there were numerous signs that the economy was becoming increasingly organized, with large aggregations of economic power in many key markets, most Americans of that generation continued to think — if they thought at all — in the individualistic terms of the eighteenth and nineteenth centuries.

It is only an accident of history that the strains of the Cold War, following upon the inflation generated by World War II and the Korean War, have raised at this particular time a serious question about the assumption underlying collective bargaining. Sooner or later, as the government strove to promote stable economic growth in order to assure high production and employment, it was inevitable that doubts would grow about the adequacy of competition as an impersonal regulator of labor and management ambitions. It was bound to become clear that just as corporations had acquired enough power to "administer" prices — that is, to set prices more or less independently of market forces — so, too, unions had become strong enough to demand unwarranted wage increases. It was also bound to dawn on government officials that big unions and corporations had achieved a privileged position that enabled them to impede and even defeat the execution of public economic policy. While the government, for instance, was using fiscal and monetary measures to check inflation, corporations and unions could be fostering it by their price and wage policies.

Obviously, these developments are forcing an evolution of collective bargaining, as well as a new relationship between government and the private sector of the economy. It is not necessary to see in this a threat to freedom. As Pope John insists in *Mater et Magistra*, government and private enterprise are both needed to insure a just, healthy, growing, and free economy (cf. nn. 56–58). What is needed are new institutions through which collaboration between government and private enterprise can take place. In this way, labor and management gain a voice in shaping the broad policies which, in the interest of the common good, they are expected to carry out. True, this is not economic freedom in the old laissez-faire sense, but it is a rich and meaningful freedom nevertheless. It offers a middle ground between detailed economic planning and an excessive, unrealistic reliance on blind, impersonal market forces. It may be the only workable democratic response to one of today's more critical demands — the need for vigorous, sustained, yet stable, economic growth.

In any discussion of government intervention in labor-management affairs, it is highly important to remember that unions and employers can do a great deal themselves to cope with new challenges to collective bargaining. Some of them have already shown commendable ingenuity in reconciling technological progress with the needs of workers for job security. One of the more interesting experiments is the cost-savings contract, already noted in Chapter 4, negotiated in 1963 by the Kaiser Steel Corporation and the United Steel-workers of America. Under this program, management is free to adopt the most efficient machines and processes its engineers can devise. Workers receive in cash a percentage of the gains in cost reduction. If their jobs are abolished, they are helped to support themselves while training for other jobs in the company.

The United Steelworkers also showed imagination in negotiating an extended vacation plan with eleven major basic steel companies led by the U. S. Steel Corporation. Every five years, half the workers covered by the contract will receive a 13-week vacation with pay. The union estimates that when the plan is fully operative, it will add 25,000 job opportunities in the industry.

The United Auto Workers and the American Motors Corporation are experimenting with a profit-sharing formula that strengthens the company's insurance programs and at the same time gives the workers a share in ownership. After an amount equal to 10 percent of the corporation's net worth is set aside, the workers receive 15 percent of the before-tax profits. In the 1961–1962 fiscal year, this amounted to $6,511,271 in cash and $3,255,636 in stock. The cash was used to finance liberalized pensions and health-insurance benefits.

These and other innovations, in the meat-packing industry, for example, and in West Coast longshoring, suggest that a growing number of employers and unions appreciate that collective bargaining, like other social institutions, must evolve to meet changing circumstances or fall by the wayside.

III

Another cloud over industrial relations is the race question — the desperate, heartbreaking demands of Negroes and other disadvantaged groups for equal job opportunities with whites. The injustice done the Negro in our economic society lies as a heavy weight on the American conscience. (It is also a grave handicap in our efforts to blunt the appeal of communism to the peoples of underdeveloped countries, most of whom are colored, and to win them to the cause of freedom and democracy.) What makes patterns of racial discrimination in employment such a galling disgrace is that they are in flagrant conflict with both our political profession and our religious faith. Although it is true that the discriminatory practices of employers and unions reflect community cultural standards — in the formation of which our churches participated, at least by their silence and acquiescence — this fact only helps to explain the injustice that has been done. It does not excuse it.

There is little point at this stage in reviewing the past and attempting to parcel out the blame between unions and employers. It is a fact that unionism is weak or nonexistent in some of the most lily-white corporations in the United States. It is also a fact that Negroes are conspicuous by their almost total absence from the ranks of higher and middle management. It is also lamentably true that antiunion employers in the South have appealed to racial prejudice to prevent the organization of their employees. Nevertheless, in a sense unions are more to blame. Their goal is not profit-seeking but justice for workers. They profess the noble purpose of defending the underdog — of improving his wages and working conditions and exacting from employers respect for his dignity as a human being. By denying their protection to Negroes, they betray the whole reason for their being.

Not all unions share in the guilt. Many of them take very seriously their solemn obligation under the AFL-CIO constitution not to discriminate by reason of race, religion, or national origin. Some of them are in the forefront of the struggle for civil rights, as is the national AFL-CIO itself. The great offenders have been the skilled craft unions on the railroads and in the building trades. Although pressures exerted by the widespread Negro demonstrations during the summer of 1963 have lowered some barriers and swept others away, it is unlikely that organized labor will be able by itself to rip out the cancer of race discrimination. The need and justification for a national fair employment practices law are self-evident. The evil will not be removed by private efforts or by state and local governments.

IV

The problems arising from racial discrimination, as well as from automation, would be easier to solve if the American economy, after a postwar surge, had not developed symptoms of hardening of the arteries. During most of the 1950's and into the 1960's, it limped rather than ran toward the goals of high production and employment. That is another cloud over unions and collective bargaining.

When job opportunities are plentiful, it is less difficult for unions to open apprenticeship programs to young recruits and to accept new machines and changes in work rules that eliminate jobs. But in recent years job openings have not been plentiful. Between 1947 and 1962, employment increased by 10 million, to a record high of 67.8 million. During the same period the working population grew even faster, by 13 million. The inevitable result was a jump in unemployment, which reached an average of four million in 1958, or 5½ percent of the workforce. It has hovered around that level ever since.

Had it not been for a surge in public employment, especially in state and local government (and there, largely in education), the record would be even worse. During the 1947–1957 decade, jobs in the private sector grew at an annual rate of 1.7 percent, or about 700,000 a year. In the course of the next five years, the rate slipped to 0.4 percent. Private employers provided only 175,000 jobs a year.

Worse still from the viewpoint of unions and the spread of collective bargaining, the increase in jobs in the private sector was concentrated in the service industries. In the goods-producing industries, where the unions have most of their strength, employment actually declined. In 1947 the goods-producing industries — agriculture, manufacturing, mining, and construction — accounted for 51 percent of total employment. The percentage plummeted to 42 in 1962. That is the reason white-collar workers now outnumber blue-collar workers in the United States.

As is well known, unions in this country, unlike those in Europe, have never had much appeal to white-collar workers, or to women, who make up a large part of the white-collar labor force. The membership of unions has been estimated at 85 percent blue-collar — a statistic that helps to explain why our 18 million unionized workers are now a smaller percen-

128 JUSTICE FOR ALL

tage of the nonfarm labor force (about 30 percent) than they
were twenty years ago.

A spurt in the economic growth rate would not automatically solve either the unemployment problem or unionism's lack of appeal to white-collar workers. It would create
an atmosphere, however, in which unions could respond more
imaginatively and dynamically to the shifting circumstances
of our times.

CHAPTER 9

People on the Land

Both Popes Leo XIII and Pius XI were mainly intent on improving the lot of urban workers in an industrial civilization — "with the redemption of non-owning workers," as Pius wrote (QA, n. 59). They may be said to have written "proletarian" encyclicals. It should be noted, however, that in defending private property Pope Leo wrote largely in terms of ownership of land (cf. RN, nn. 11–17). Indeed, this seems to be the type of ownership he encouraged as the chief means of freeing workers from total dependence on wage income (cf. nn. 65–66).

In *Quadragesimo Anno*, Pius XI referred only a few times to agriculture. Observing that the majority of men still earn their living on the land (cf. n. 102), he deplored the condition of "the huge army of rural workers, pushed to the lowest level of existence and deprived of all hope of ever acquiring 'some property in land'" (n. 59). In an interesting paragraph, he pointed out the connection between full employment and a "right proportion in the prices at which goods are sold that are produced by the various occupations, such as agriculture, manufacturing and others" (n. 75). The Pope was aware that a catastrophic drop in farm prices contributed to the depression of the 1930's and helped to prolong it.

With Pope Pius XII, we note some shift in emphasis in the Church's social teaching from industry to agriculture. In a radio address on Pentecost, 1941, the Pope repeated an idea found in *Rerum Novarum*, that of all types of private property "none is more conformable to nature than the land, the holding on which the family lives, and from the products of which it draws all or part of its subsistence." In an audience granted to Italian farmers on November 15, 1946, he praised their stability and capacity to resist critical shocks to society. At a time when Europe was groping its way back to some semblance of order after World War II, he warned them against greed and the urban vice of subordinating human needs to the profitable employment of capital.

Later on in his pontificate, the Pope grew concerned over the use of capitalistic techniques in agriculture. He conceded that these had expanded farm production, but he was fearful that they might alter the character of rural living by making the countryside a mere expansion of the city. Marxism, with its "idolatrous worship of technology and industrialization," professedly aims at this goal, he said, so that the countryside is "reduced to nothing more than a reserve of manpower for industrial production." But economic liberalism, "once the pursuit of gain on the part of finance capitalism bears with all its weight upon economic life," also brings about the same result. Because of the spiritual, as well as economic, values inherent in work in the fields, the Pope insisted that farm technology be subordinated to man (To the International Catholic Congress on Rural Problems, July 2, 1951). In his view, "keeping within the spirit of the social doctrine of the Church," farming is more than an economic activity aimed at making a profit; it is a noble way of life eminently suited to strengthen the family — a "bulwark of sound liberty, a protective dike against the danger of urbanism, and an effective contribution to the continuation of the sound traditions of the people" (Address on Problems of Rural Life, September 18, 1957).

With Pope John, the son of Italian peasants, the Church's teaching on agriculture, which had been evolving through the work of such professional groups as our own National Catholic Rural Life Conference, was expanded and systematized. He became the first pope to deal comprehensively with farming in an encyclical.

I

This new accent in the Church's social doctrine was very timely. Not only was agriculture undergoing the same technological revolution in the 1950's that a century and a half earlier had changed the face of industry, but there was abroad almost everywhere in rural society a disturbing spirit of unrest and dissatisfaction. This malaise was impelling millions to flee the land for already crowded metropolitan centers.

Always the realist, even when preaching lofty ideals, Pope John understood that some of this migration was inevitable. "We all know," he wrote, "that as an economy develops and flourishes, the labor force in agriculture decreases," while at the same time "the percentage of the labor force employed in industry and the services rises" (MM, n. 124). But the Pope knew also that other causes lay behind the headlong flight from the land, and these grievously distressed him. He mentioned the desire to escape from a confining and unpromising environment, a longing for novelty and adventure, greed for quickly amassed riches, and a yearning for a more comfortable way of life. The story, he said, was the same almost everywhere: productivity in agriculture had fallen behind productivity in other sectors of the economy, with the result that rural living standards were lower than those prevailing in the cities.

Obviously, then, if large-scale migration from the land was to be checked, something had to be done to right this imbalance. The disproportion in productivity had to be narrowed and the living standards of the rural-farm population raised. Farmers must be helped to appreciate again the nobility of their work, so interesting in its variety, so necessary to their fellowmen, so "rich in allusions to God, the Creator and Provider." They must be persuaded that they can develop their personalities no less richly in the country than in the city, and they must be enabled at the same time to look with confidence to the future (cf. nn. 124–125, 144).

To assist in achieving these goals, Pope John made a number of recommendations.

First, the Pope said, there must be the necessary structure in rural regions for decent, civilized living. This means that the government, especially, ought to be concerned about providing good roads, means of communication, health facilities, elementary education, opportunities for technical training, water, power, and other services needed for modern homes. There must be provision, too, for religious practice and recreation (cf. n. 127).

In the second place, public policy ought to aim at a balanced development of the economy. Agriculture must be helped to make use of all scientific advances and technological developments, so that it can keep pace with improvements in industry and the services (cf. n. 128).

More specifically, governments should promote a balanced development of the economy by appropriate policies on taxes, credit, social insurance, and prices (cf. n. 131). Taxes ought to bear less heavily on farm income than on other types of income. Special institutions should make credit available on suitable terms, since agricultural investment is not as attractive to capital as other investments. There should be crop insurance, as well as a system of social security for farmers and their families; and the benefits paid under the social-security system, despite smaller contributions by farmers, should not be substantially lower than those paid to other groups. Because of the nature of agricultural production, farm prices must be protected against the vagaries of the market. While farm products, since they satisfy primary needs, should be so priced that they are within reach of all consumers, this is no excuse "for compelling a whole class of citizens to live in a permanent state of socio-economic inferiority" (n. 140).

Since agricultural production is organized in different ways in different countries, Pope John notes that "it is impossible to determine a priori what the structure of farm enterprises ought to be." Nevertheless, since the family-type farm responds so well to the human and religious needs of people, it ought to be fostered and encouraged as much as possible (cf. n. 142).

This recommendation must not be confused with a romantic outlook on agriculture that ignores the realities of twentieth-century life. If the family farm is to survive in this technological age, the Pope writes realistically, "it must produce sufficient income to enable the family to live in decent comfort." That implies that it must aim not only at producing efficiently, using up-to-date methods, but also at distributing its products in a rewarding way (cf. n. 143). In other words, family-type farmers must organize on both the economic and political level if they are to maintain their position in modern society. The individual farmer, with his limited resources, like the individual worker, is at the mercy of the market:

> One should remember that in agriculture, as in every other sector of production, association is a vital need. This is especially so where family-type farms are involved. Rural workers should feel a sense of solidarity one with another, and should unite to form co-operatives and vocational associations. Both types of organization are very necessary if farmers are to benefit from scientific and technical progress in methods of production. The same is true if they are to contribute effectively toward maintaining the prices of their products, or if they are to attain an equal footing with other economic and professional classes, which are also usually organized. Then, too, if farmers organize, they can exercise an influence on the conduct of public affairs proportionate to their status (n. 146).

Like trade unions, business associations, and professional groups of all kinds, farm organizations should not pursue the interests of their members without due regard for the interests of other classes. They must be ready when the need arises to subordinate their individual and group interests to the common good. Only when they act in this responsible way have they a right to demand of government that it assist their efforts to survive and prosper (cf. n. 147).

II

From one point of view, what Pope John says about farming can be read in terms of broad approval of the philosophy that has shaped most American thinking about agriculture and has long dominated public policy.

Heir of a tradition of Western thought that goes back to Aristotle, Thomas Jefferson saw in a healthy farm class a bulwark of democracy. To him the family farm was the nursery of all the virtues — independence, self-reliance, personal initiative, industriousness, hard work — on which freedom depends. Many other great Americans, including Theodore Roosevelt, whose name will always be connected with the conservation movement in this country, shared Jefferson's conviction. One of the great pioneers of the Catholic social movement in the United States, Msgr. John A. Ryan, spoke for many of his fellow citizens, regardless of religious belief, when he wrote:

> As a rule country life is more nearly normal than urban life. The farm provides a better environment for the cultivation of the fundamental virtues, for healthy family conditions, for a sane outlook on life, for a proper sense of relative values, and for the development of independence, self-respect and self-reliance. Farm life is much less likely than urban life to produce and develop the slave mind (A Better Economic Order, p. 155).

More recently, President Eisenhower testified to the nation's abiding faith in the value of farming pursued as a way of life as well as a business. In a special message to Congress on January 9, 1956, he wrote: "In America, agriculture is more than an industry; it is a way of life. Throughout our history the family farm has given strength and vitality to our entire social order. We must keep it healthy and vigorous."

As for public policy on agriculture, the federal and state governments have already done practically all that Pope John recommends. The rural regions of the United States are crisscrossed by ribbons of steel and concrete. It is a rare and remote farm nowadays that doesn't have access to electricity. No other class in our society has so easily and abundantly available the latest scientific and technological research as have our farmers. They also have special credit facilities, and enjoy price protection for a number of key crops. Our farm owners and their families are incorporated in the social-security system. If in some regions their health facilities, housing, and education are still not up to city standards, the reason, surely, is not that the government is unconcerned about balanced economic growth, or has done nothing to make rural living as pleasant and rewarding as urban living. As we saw in Chapter 6, agriculture is a $5 billion item in the federal budget.

With regard to the political influence Pope John says farmers ought to have, one can only say that in this country, on both state and federal levels, agriculture is overrepresented in the legislatures rather than underrepresented. In the federal establishment, the Department of Agriculture is easily one of the largest agencies.

Nor is there any lack of strong private organizations to defend agriculture's political and economic interests. The American Farm Bureau Federation, the National Grange, the National Farmers Union, and the Nation Council of Farmer Cooperatives are only the best known among dozens of thriving farm groups.

In all these respects, and in others besides, the concern shown for agriculture in the United States seems to fulfill the recommendations of *Mater et Magistra*.

III

From another point of view, however, Pope John's encyclical doesn't have much pertinence to the American scene. Two of the great farm problems of today, the Pope says, are inequalities both in productive efficiency and in living standards between the agricultural sector and the industrial and service sectors. But in this country, while there is some inequality in living standards between rural and urban groups, as we shall see, there is no inequality whatsoever in productive efficiency. On the contrary, if we use output per man-hour of work as the criterion, agriculture has made faster progress over the past quarter century than any other sector of the economy.

This progress has been truly breathtaking. In a Twentieth Century Fund study published in 1963, *Farms and Farmers in an Urban Age*, Professor Edward Higbee of the University of Rhode Island hits some of the high spots. It took 20 man-hours of work, even with a horse-drawn reaper, to harvest an acre of wheat in 1880. It takes less than 2 man-hours today. A mechanical picker on one of our big Southwest cotton farms does the work of 40 men. With modern equipment a single farmer can load 10 tons of hay an hour. During World War II two farmers pitching hay a whole afternoon could not have done that much. In 1910, it took 147 man-hours of work to raise 100 bushels of corn. On the most efficient farms in the corn belt, it takes today less than 4 hours. Nor has the technological revolution stopped with the big grain and cotton crops. Anyone who has seen huge, ingenious machines moving slowly down rows of lettuce in California, or rows of potatoes in Wisconsin, or topping and pulling radishes by the acre, must wonder why some people still bother to tend backyard gardens.

The overall figures on gains in agricultural efficiency are scarcely less impressive. In 1940, one farmer grew enough food to support 11 persons. Twenty years later, equipped with new pesticides, fertilizers and machines, he fed 26 persons. (Between 1917 and 1960, the number of tractors on U. S. farms increased from 51,000 to five million.) Output per man-hour in industry rose 25.5 percent between 1948 and 1957; it jumped 48.6 percent in agriculture. If we take the 1950's alone, the comparison is even more striking. The average annual increase in production per worker in agriculture was a little more than 6 percent; it was less than 3 percent outside of agriculture. Businessmen like to boast about the amount of capital it takes to finance a job in industry. It does take a lot — $15,900 per worker in 1960. But that same year investment per worker in agriculture was $21,300.

From a technological standpoint, agriculture is most emphatically not the neglected sector that Pope John describes.

What the Pope says, however, about disparity in incomes is amply verified in the United States. Our vast technological progress in agriculture has not been translated into monetary rewards. For more than thirty years, beginning with the Hoover administration, the federal government has been striving, at considerable expense, to bring about parity of income between farmers and city folk. Except for brief periods when wartime demand placed a firm foundation under farm prices, it has only partially succeeded. From a high of $17.8 billion in 1948, farm proprietors' income dropped to a low of $11.4 billion in 1959; in 1962, it was $13.3 billion. Government payments to farmers, mostly under price-support and conservation programs, accounted for much of the income gain between 1959 and 1962. They increased during that period from $3.5 billion to a little over $5 billion.

For several reasons, though, this picture is not quite so bad as it appears.

In the first place, it costs more in the city to maintain a given standard of living than it does on the farm. Some authorities estimate that farmers need only 65 percent of urban incomes to live on a comparable level. In 1959, the average annual income of farm families from agriculture ($2,875) was only 48 percent of the average income of nonfarm families ($5,911). However, many farmers had supplementary income that year from part-time jobs off the farm. When this is included, the average income of farm families rises to $5,115 in 1959, or about 87 percent of the income of nonfarm families.

In the second place, farm operators' income is being divided every year among a declining number of families. The number of farms in the country dropped from 6.8 million in 1940 to 3.7 million in 1961. Over the same period, farm population fell by more than 10 million.

In the third place, although the growth of farm income has been stagnant, the rise of farm values has been exceptionally rapid. In 1940, the value of all the farm land and buildings in the nation was $33.6 billion; in 1959 it was $128.9 billion.

Between 1950 and 1960 alone, the average value of an acre of farm land jumped from $65 to $120. Nor are farm holdings heavily mortgaged. In 1960, mortgage debt came to only 10 percent of farm real-estate values.

Nevertheless, even though many farm families could realize sizable capital gains by selling out, the fact remains that perhaps as many as two thirds of our farm families earn inadequate incomes from agriculture. In 1961, a fourth of them had annual incomes below $2,000. More than half had incomes below $4,000.

IV

Yet, as was said above, the nation's farm policy has aimed for many years now at giving farmers a fair share of the national income. The chief instrument of that policy has been a system of price supports by which farmers are guaranteed something approaching a parity price for their products — a price, that is, which is deemed fair relative to the prices that farmers pay for labor, equipment, and living needs. If the market price for a commodity is lower than the support price fixed by the government, farmers can hand over their crops on loan to the Agriculture Department's Commodity Credit Corporation. CCC pays them the support price. Should the market price subsequently rise above the support price, farmers can reclaim their crops and dispose of them through normal channels of trade. If the market price does not rise and farmers don't reclaim their crops, CCC obtains title to them and they become part of the national reserve.

To maintain the support price and at the same time to prevent an accumulation of huge surpluses, the government imposes acreage and marketing controls as a condition for price supports. To make these restrictions on the farmer's freedom more palatable, it pays him something for idling his acres and for participating in conservation programs.

For a number of years the nation's farm-price policy, aided by worldwide shortages of food and fiber during and after

World War II, worked tolerably well. It bolstered farm income and cost the government only relatively small amounts of money. Nor did city folk have much to complain about. Their burden as taxpayers of supporting farm prices was not very heavy. As consumers, they had to spend only a fifth of their incomes on food — a lower percentage than any other people in the world has to spend. In recent years, however, as surpluses mounted, the cost of the farm program has skyrocketed. In the fiscal year beginning July 1, 1961, the Department of Agriculture spent $5.8 billion subsidizing farmers, of which $4.5 billion went to stabilize farm prices. That was a sharp contrast with fiscal 1954, when the department spent only $1.6 billion to bolster prices, and its total outlays on farmers came to no more than $2.5 billion.

By the summer of 1962, as a consequence of the enormous productivity of U. S. farms, the Commodity Credit Corporation had acquired inventories of surplus grain and dairy products valued at $4.6 billion. To store and insure this hoard was costing the government a million dollars a day. By that time it had become painfully evident in Washington that a drastic change of some kind had to be made. If farmers were to continue enjoying high price supports, they would have to accept much stricter controls over their freedom to plant and market.

V

Some years earlier, the National Catholic Rural Life Conference had begun to have doubts about the price-support program. More and more the program was assuming the character of a crusade against abundance. The Conference understood, of course, that it is not easy to reconcile agricultural abundance with a just return to farmers for their productive energies. Unlike the businessman, the farmer cannot shut down his plant when inventories hang heavily over the market. He cannot tell the cow to stop giving milk, the hens to cease laying eggs, the wheat and corn to quit growing. He cannot readily shift his product to meet changes in demand. He cannot control his price, as many businessmen can and do control their prices. The more the farmer produces, the less he is apt to receive for his product.

The Rural Life Conference knew all this. But it also knew that abundance is a blessing, and that no program designed to protect farm income from uncontrolled market forces was acceptable if it treated abundance as a curse.

If all the people of the world enjoyed a decent diet, fear of abundance might make some sense. It might even be justified as a guiding motive of agricultural policy. But how could it possibly make sense, not only to a Christian, but to any normal, God-fearing man, when a sizable part of the world's peoples didn't know what it was to have a square meal, and went to sleep every night hungry? How could it make sense when communism was sweeping through Asia and threatening Africa and Latin America on the strength of a promise to give land to the peasants and to the suffering, nameless masses a better break in life?

At its annual convention in October, 1954, at Davenport, Iowa, the Rural Life Conference took a momentous step. After sober deliberation, the delegates approved a resolution that put them in open opposition to the nation's restrictionist farm program. The statement began on a solemnly religious note:

> The NCRLC is deeply grateful to Almighty God for the abundant production of food and fiber during 1954 in the United States. His fruitful blessing has been placed on the difficult and devoted work of our farmers and has brought it to success. This year again there is true cause for thanksgiving.

Further emphasizing their break with the dominant thinking in Washington, which had put into effect additional acreage cuts and stricter curbs on marketing, the delegates noted with warm approval "the trend toward increased production per acre and per person." They called the gain in productivity, which partly canceled the intended effects of the acreage cuts, "a special gift from God and a source of added wealth to the nation." Finally, as if to make doubly sure that nobody missed the point, the delegates added this paragraph:

> We regret to hear from many voices in this country a growing chorus of alarm over what is called "surplus" production. We believe that the concern is misplaced. The real matter for alarm is that the "surplus" is not recognized as a great blessing and a rare opportunity.

The delegates to the Conference did not stop there, however. They had no wish to be identified with those critics of the national farm program who want to end all government intervention and return to a free market in farm products, regardless of social consequences. They wanted to make clear their agreement with the proponents of price-support, restricted-production programs that farmers labor under special handicaps which require government help. Without aid of some kind, they cannot obtain a fair share of the national income. Yet, in return for discharging their social duty of producing food and fiber, they have a moral right to a fair income. The fact that "present methods of price support have neither satisfied the consumer and taxpayer nor solved the major problems which beset the farmer" must not be used as an argument for exposing farmers to the full force of the law of supply and demand. Rather it is an argument for a "fundamentally new approach" to the farm problem.

A new approach should be fair, of course, to consumers as well as farmers. It should encourage, not discourage, production. It should be practical; that is, it should blunt the effects of the law of supply and demand but not try to repeal it.

Was such an approach available? The delegates thought that it was. They recommended, as "a more workable solution" than price supports and one with less of a bias toward bigness, a system of "carefully planned direct subsidies to farmers."

The system would work in this way. Farmers would produce anything they liked, and as much as they liked. They would sell their products in an uncontrolled market, where prices were set by supply and demand. Meanwhile, the government would compute the parity price for each product. The difference would then be ascertained between the parity price and the price the farmer received for his product when he brought it to market. This difference the government would pay to the farmer as a direct subsidy.

The Rural Life Conference did not believe, however, that the government ought to subsidize the total production of American agriculture. It wanted the law to distinguish sharply between family farms and "factories in the fields." "We feel," said the delegates at Davenport, "that no subsidies should be paid on operations which exceed a specified maximum number of units." For anything over the maximum, the big, commercial farmers would receive no more than the market price.

Under a system of cash payments determined by the differential between market prices and parity prices, the production of some farm commodities — notably wheat, corn, and cotton — might be expected to increase substantially, since all curbs on planting and marketing would be removed. Would not such a policy lead to even more burdensome surpluses than we have today?

The Rural Life Conference anticipated this objection by calling for a more liberal foreign-trade program. We stand, said the delegates, "for the gradual and progressive removal of tariff and other obstacles to trade among nations." They wanted our surplus products to flow freely through world trade channels to people who needed them. Despite generous American help to many nations during the entire postwar period, the Rural Life Conference was persuaded that we could do more. We have surpluses, it said, because we still do not fully appreciate that we are, under God, stewards of our rich natural resources, not absolute owners. Admittedly, the problem of world distribution of farm commodities was extraordinarily difficult, but surely it was not insoluble. The Rural Life Conference did not claim to have all the answers. It was certain only that the present policy of restricting farm production when the world's population is growing and unnumbered millions are hungry or starving is painfully anomalous and possibly immoral.

Nor was it only the restrictionism of the price-support approach that raised doubts in the minds of the Rural Life Conference. As the government's program developed, it came to favor, contrary to the intentions of many sponsors of the law, the big, corporation farms over family-type farms. The principal beneficiaries of price-support loans, for instance, turned out to be large-scale farmers, some of whom have pocketed more than a million dollars of government money a year. At the other end of the scale, the 56 percent of the nation's farms which are considered small or marginal regularly receive less than 7 percent of government payments.

The Rural Life Conference's plan for direct cash payments limited to a specified number of units would undoubtedly tend to right this imbalance in government subsidies. It would also be popular, we might add, with that vast majority of Americans who must earn their daily bread and work out their salvation in an urban environment. Under the price-support program, city people now pay twice to assure farmers an adequate income — once at the grocery store and meat market in the form of artificially high prices, and again in the form of taxes at the Bureau of Internal Revenue. They would pay only once under a program of cash subsidies — in the form of taxes. Their food bills would be lower, although the saving — since even now the farmer receives only 40 cents of the consumer's food dollar — would be less than is popularly imagined.

VI

It should be noted, however, that a program of direct cash subsidies might not significantly improve the lot of small, marginal farmers. There were 1,640,910 farms in 1959 valued at $2,500 or less. They contributed only 5.3 percent to the total value of all farm sales. Whether they can, or ought to be, saved as commercial undertakings — some of them are not commercial undertakings now and are doubtfully classified as farms — is an

open question. In an age when huge amounts of capital investment are required for successful farm operations, it is hard to
see how they can be made viable. They produce so little that
no feasible level of subsidies or farm prices would be high
enough to enable them to make ends meet. In view of Pope
John's observation, noted earlier in this chapter, that "if a
family-type farm is to survive, it must produce sufficient income
to enable the family to live in decent comfort," there appears
to be no compelling moral or social reason why these marginal
farmers must be kept afloat. Society is obliged, however, to
help them shift to more rewarding work and to adjust to urban
ways of living.

This judgment does not appear to be out of line with the
thinking of the National Catholic Rural Life Conference.

At its 1956 convention in Sioux Falls, South Dakota, the
Conference reiterated its support of the family farm. If weighty
economic, cultural, and religious considerations dictated the
preservation of the family farm in 1923, when the National
Catholic Rural Life Conference was founded, these were no
less imperative thirty years later.

The convention delegates went to some trouble, however, to
explain precisely what it is they were defending. They were not
necessarily defending small farms. They were certainly not
defending marginal farms — farms which probably never could
offer to a family anything but a bare subsistence. Rather they
were defending "a socio-economic institution in which the capital, labor, and management of the family is organized toward
the production of food and fiber for the benefit of the family
and society."

In somewhat less technical language this means a farm
owned by the family working it. It means a farm on which the
members of the family do most of the work, with a minimum
of hired help. It means a farm that gives a family an income
fully adequate for the family's support. It means a farm of
varying size, depending on what it produces and where it is

located. It may mean 10 acres for a family operating a truck farm in New Jersey, but 100 acres for a family on a dairy farm in Wisconsin. For a family raising corn and hogs in Iowa, it may mean as much as 250 acres.

In supporting the family farm, the National Catholic Rural Life Conference is not trying to return to the simpler forms of a vanished age. It recognizes, as does Pope John, that science and technology have revolutionized farm production, and that the end is not yet in sight. The great benefits of this revolution are already obvious in increased production and an easier life for many farmers. The conference welcomes this progress. It insists only that man remain the master of technological change. Not all the consequences of the agricultural revolution, it says, are unmixed blessings. To the extent, for instance, that the present trend toward fewer and larger farms represents the amalgamation of small, marginal units, it is good; but to the extent that it reflects the merging of farms already adequate in size, it is bad. It will remain the policy of the National Catholic Rural Life Conference, therefore (and probably of the country as well), to preserve the economically viable family-size farm.

VII

In *Mater et Magistra*, Pope John linked the survival of family farms to the establishment of a "flourishing system of co-operatives" (n. 143). This idea is not without considerable private and public support in the United States. The theory is that consumer or purchasing co-ops increase the farmer's income by helping him to buy cheaply many products needed for farm and home. Marketing co-ops strengthen his bargaining position in the market and enable him to demand a better price for his commodities.

Until now, our 9000 farm consumer and marketing co-ops have not been a major influence in U. S. agriculture. Marketing co-ops are largely confined to dairying and such specialty crops as rice, nuts, fruits, and vegetables. They do operate in a limited way, however, in poultry, livestock, cotton and wool, dry beans, peas, tobacco, and sugar products. All told, co-ops market about $10 billion worth of farm products a year.

Co-ops may have a great future, however. At the present time, the price-support program for wheat is undergoing a crisis of sorts. Farmers are rebelling against the stricter production controls that the government believes necessary to cope with mounting surpluses. Should the price-support program be abandoned, co-ops may impress a growing number of farmers as a workable alternative. Before this happens, though, Congress may have to amend the antitrust laws to insure the legality of co-op marketing techniques aimed at influencing prices. Such a development would be very much in accord with the recommendation in *Mater et Magistra* that price protection for farm products "be primarily the work of the interested parties," with the government acting in a watchdog capacity (n. 137).

Throughout this chapter, the word "farmer" has been used to mean "farm operator," whether owner or tenant. To complete the picture, it is necessary to add something about hired farm workers in the United States.

They are a small part of the labor force, totaling only 1,817,000 men and women in 1962. They are also a declining part of the labor force, both absolutely and relatively. (There were 2,679,000 hired farm workers in 1940.) One tenth of them are Mexican nationals (*braceros*) who are brought every year to the United States to work on farms in the West and Southwest. A quarter of them are domestic migrant workers, largely Negroes and Mexican-Americans from Florida and Texas. The majority of these workers are poorly paid by industry standards. This is especially true of the migrants, who in 1961 earned $6.70 a day and $1,039 a year on the average. In many cases the housing and health facilities of hired farm hands are grossly inadequate. They are not protected by the nation's labor laws, and their employers bitterly, and successfully, resist unionization. The migrants among them are the truly forgotten people in our affluent society. Their plight is a disgrace to the 5 percent of U. S. farmers who employ them. It is a blot on the record of the Congress, which has done very little to help them. It is an abrasive challenge to the conscience of a nation that still considers itself God-fearing and Christian.

CHAPTER 10

Rich and Poor Nations

Perhaps nowhere in the world's literature is the contrast between rich and poor painted so simply and powerfully as in our Lord's parable of Dives and Lazarus. Nowhere is the divine displeasure with unfeeling, self-centered affluence more eloquently phrased. As we read in St. Luke:

> There was a certain rich man who used to clothe himself in purple and fine linen, and who feasted every day in splendid fashion. And there was a certain poor man, named Lazarus, who lay at his gate, covered with sores, and longing to be filled with the crumbs that fell from the rich man's table; even the dogs would come and lick his sores. And it came to pass that the poor man died and was borne away by the angels into Abraham's bosom; but the rich man also died and was buried in hell (Lk 16:19–22).

As we have repeatedly seen, all the modern Popes who have dealt with the social question have deplored the inequitable distribution of wealth and income in the modern world. Popes Leo XIII and Pius XI were chiefly intent on narrowing the huge, divisive gap that had opened during the nineteenth century between a relatively small capitalist class and, to quote Pope Leo, "the unnumbered masses of non-owning workers" (RN, n. 6). With Popes Pius XII and John XXIII, this concern was broadened to include imbalances between agriculture and industry, between different regions of the same country, and between the rich and poor nations of the world. As Pope John wrote in *Mater et Magistra:*

> The historical evolution of human affairs brings into ever greater relief the fact that the demands of justice and equity have a bearing not only on relations between dependent workingmen and contractors or employers, but also on relations between

different economic sectors, between areas economically more advanced and those that are underdeveloped within the same nation, and, from a world point of view, on relations among countries at different stages of socioeconomic development (n. 122).

I

There have always been rich and poor nations in the world, but until almost yesterday vast distances kept the two apart. The poor nations endured their fate as something that was customary and inevitable. Most residents of rich nations went their relatively comfortable ways scarcely aware of poverty elsewhere. The world was one, but only a few seemed to realize it. Each nation lived unto itself, with little sense of obligation to a larger community.

Now all this is changing, and changing very rapidly. Of the many breath-taking developments and inventions that have rocked the world over the past quarter century, few are so fraught with grave consequences to the future of the human race as the revolution in communications and transport. The world has suddenly become a single, vast neighborhood.

Throughout his pontificate, Pope Pius XII, well aware of "the historical evolution of human affairs" mentioned by Pope John, and tirelessly intent on peace, strove to impress this on his contemporaries. In his first encyclical, *Summi Pontificatus*, issued only a few weeks after the outbreak of World War II, he sounded a note that recurs time and time again in his allocutions and radio discourses:

A disposition, in fact, of the divinely sanctioned natural order divides the human race into social groups, nations or states, which are mutually independent in organization and in the direction of their internal life. But for all that, the human race is bound together by reciprocal ties, moral and juridical, into a great commonwealth directed to the good of all nations and ruled by special laws which protect its unity and promote its prosperity.

No one can fail to see how the claim of absolute autonomy for the state stands in open opposition to this natural law that is inherent in man — nay, denies it utterly — and, therefore, leaves the stability of international relations at the mercy of the will of rulers, while it destroys the possibility of true union and fruitful collaboration directed to the general good.

Eighteen years later, near the end of his reign, with the world living precariously in the deadly shadow of a man-made mushroom cloud, he was still reminding men that "in God's plan every man is his neighbor's brother, every people a member in the family of nations, which forms a single community destined for a common end, with solemn, social obligations resting on all" (Address to Atlantic Treaty Association, June 27, 1957).

On a number of occasions, Pope Pius XII emphasized the economic consequences of the drawing together of nations in space and time. In his radio message on Christmas Eve, 1941, in which he listed the moral requirements of a just and lasting peace, he said:

> Within the limits of a new order founded on moral principles there is no place for that cold and calculating egoism which tends to hoard economic resources and materials destined for the use of all, to such an extent that the nations less favored by nature are not permitted access to them. . . . If in the future peace this point were not to be courageously dealt with, there would remain in the relations between peoples a deep and far-reaching root blossoming forth into bitter dissensions and burning jealousies, which would lead eventually to new conflicts.

In an address on December 8, 1953, to delegates attending the seventh session of the UN Food and Agricultural Organization, the Pope lamented that despite a vast effort to help underfed peoples, "who make up seventy per cent of the world's population," the problem "seems to become larger and more complicated the more one works at it." Worse still, the imbalance between the "haves" and "have-nots" in the world community was increasing:

> It is a fact, in spite of recent improvements, that the problem of food remains a crucial one for a large part of mankind. As you state in your reports, the present situation of the world, from an agricultural point of view, is characterized by a marked

imbalance between developed areas and countries which are still insufficiently developed. In the first case, production is increasing rapidly, the level of consumption is rising again and exports are mounting; in the other — particularly in the Far East — production remains inadequate, food insufficient and imports limited. The possibility of famine, with its frightful consequences, unceasingly haunts millions of men, a period of drought being enough to bring about that terrible calamity. Moreover, it is necessary to take account of the continuous growth of the population, which demands, at the risk of making the evil worse, a parallel increase in the goods to be consumed.

This being the case in a world become a neighborhood, "no one possesses the spirit of Christ," Pope Pius XII told the Catholic World Health Congress on July 27, 1958, "who does not share the worries of all his brothers, wherever they may live, or whatever their race may be, nor who does not ardently desire to provide them with advantages still reserved to certain privileged countries."

Such was the teaching that Pope John XXIII confirmed and developed in *Mater et Magistra*. The main principles, derived from Scripture and the natural law, stand out clearly: all men are brothers, children of a common Father; since nations, though autonomous, are not sovereign in an absolute sense, they must serve the international common good; under present circumstances, this good requires that imbalances between rich and poor nations be lessened; rich nations are obliged, therefore, in justice and charity, to help poor nations raise their living standards.

II

Pope John begins his treatment of justice and charity among nations with a simple statement of fact:

> One of the most difficult problems facing the modern world concerns relations between nations that are economically advanced and those in the earlier stages of development. The former enjoy a high standard of living, while the latter suffer from extreme poverty (n. 157).

To Pope John, mindful of his role of Universal Father, the mere statement of the problem suggests the answer:

The solidarity which binds all men and makes them members, in a sense, of the same family requires that nations enjoying an abundance of material goods should not remain indifferent to those nations whose citizens suffer from internal problems that result in poverty, hunger and an inability to enjoy even the more elementary human rights (n. 157).

Then the Pope solemnly repeated words that he had spoken earlier (on May 3, 1960) to the directors of the UN Food and Agricultural Organization: "It is necessary to awaken men's consciences to a sense of the responsibility which weighs upon everyone, especially upon those who are more richly endowed with this world's goods"; for "we are all equally responsible for the undernourished peoples. . . ."

The moral obligation to help underdeveloped countries, the Pope adds, is especially urgent today because of "the growing interdependence among nations." In the shrunken world of the twentieth century, "contemporary problems of any importance, whatever their content may be — scientific, technical, economic, social, political or cultural — today commonly present supranational and often global dimensions" (n. 201). Therefore, the Pope concludes, "it is impossible to preserve a lasting and beneficial peace while glaring socio-economic inequalities persist among them" (n. 157). The security of the rich is menaced by the insecurity of the poor.

(Although Pope John, in his characteristically positive approach to world problems, did not mention the threat of communism as a motive for assisting poor nations, this, too, is a legitimate reason. If we truly love all the people of the world, as Christians must, we ought to be prepared to help them resist the temptation, born sometimes of desperation and despair, to barter their freedom for economic aid.)

As Pope John explains, the developing countries of the world need more than one-shot, emergency aid. They do need foodstuffs, of course, and clothing and medicine to satisfy the immediate needs of their hungry and diseased people. But if they are to remove the deep-rooted causes of their misery and raise their standards of living, they also require vast amounts of capital and almost unlimited technical assistance. To be effective, this help must be offered on a long-term basis (cf. nn. 161–163). The Pope takes the occasion to applaud what public and private agencies have already done to help underdeveloped countries to help themselves (cf. nn. 164–165). He is especially gratified at the response of Catholics in the wealthy nations, who through such organizations as our own Catholic Relief Services, N.C.W.C., Papal Volunteers, and Aid for International Development have contributed not only food, clothing, and medicine, but educational and technical assistance to their needy brothers all over the world (cf. n. 183).

Well aware that much more remains to be done to lessen imbalances among nations, the Pope felt it necessary to offer "some reflections and words of caution" for both the givers and receivers of foreign aid.

The developing countries, learning from the mistakes of the wealthy nations, should take care that "social progress keep pace with economic development." It is obviously necessary to concentrate on increasing the national product, but it is no less necessary, Pope John warns, and conformable to justice "that the riches produced be equitably distributed among all citizens." The Pope is also insistent on balanced development, with equal attention paid to industry, agriculture, and services (cf. n. 168).

To these "words of caution" most administrators of the U. S. foreign-aid program would probably murmur a heartfelt "Amen." In many underdeveloped countries the rich are few and the poor many, and the distance between them is explosively great. In too many cases, the rich show little enthusiasm for social progress as Pope John defines it, since social progress requires a redistribution of national wealth and income. To go no farther away from home, in some Latin-American countries the rich are so wedded to the status quo that the Alliance for

Progress is falling short of its targets. Blinded by their narrow, immediate self-interest, these people risk losing everything in the long run. For the only alternative to social change today in underdeveloped countries is likely to be violent revolution. What happened in Cuba could easily happen in a half-dozen other Latin-American lands.

For the rest, Pope John fully identifies the Church with "the revolution of rising expectations," although he reminds men that material well-being is not the supreme goal of life. Scientific and technological progress, economic development, and an increase in living standards are all worthy objectives. They make "a positive contribution to human civilization." But they would be purchased at too dear a price if they destroyed the consciousness of those higher, spiritual values that are the foundation of a truly human culture (cf. nn. 175–176).

In giving aid to the developing countries, therefore, the rich nations must be careful not to export a materialistic philosophy along with their food, money, and technology. Furthermore, they should respect native cultures and not yield "to the temptation of imposing their own way of life" on the recipient peoples. Finally, the wealthy nations should avoid the even greater temptation of using their aid for "their own profit or imperialistic aggrandizement" (nn. 169–171). On this point, the Holy Father writes very bluntly:

> If such an attempt be made, it must be explicitly labeled an effort to introduce a new form of colonialism, which, however cleverly disguised, would be only a repetition of that old, outdated type from which many peoples have recently escaped. It would have, too, a harmful impact on international relations and constitute a threat to world peace (n. 172).

III

Perhaps no part of *Mater et Magistra* has been read more attentively in the United States than this section on relations between developed and underdeveloped countries. In one way or another, by loans or grants, the American people have spent about $100 billion on foreign military and economic aid since the end of World War II. They have done so for the most part uncomplainingly, partly because they felt morally obliged to help other peoples, and partly because they saw in foreign aid an expression of enlightened self-interest. Whatever strengthened the free world, they reasoned, whatever helped to contain the communist drive for world domination, contributed to world peace and the security of the United States.

In recent years, however, these mixed motives have been losing some of their appeal. Critics of foreign-aid programs are now listened to with growing respect and sympathy. A large section of the daily press beats the editorial drums for substantial cutbacks in spending. Congress is increasingly reluctant to vote the annual appropriations requested by the President. For its part, the public is discouraged by evidence of waste in some of the programs, by what it regards as a lack of gratitude on the part of recipient countries, by the absence of striking successes comparable to the postwar recovery of Western Europe under the Marshall Plan. Many are plainly tired of carrying the rich man's burden. As far as they can peer into the future, they see no end to the expense of foreign aid.

Yet the fundamental need for foreign aid — to lessen the scandalous imbalance between rich and poor nations — remains as urgent as ever. The moral obligation, as Pope John insists, still presses on us. For all over the world, hundreds of millions of human beings, our brothers, continue to languish in ignorance, disease, and poverty. Worse still, the gap between the rich and poor countries, despite large injections of aid, is widening, not narrowing. Between 1948 and 1961, according to a UN study, *The Growth of World Industry, 1938–1961*, per-capita output in the developing nations rose from $100 to $135. Over the same span, per-capita output in industrialized countries jumped from $1,040 to $1,480.

It may help us to see this persisting challenge in more meaningful terms if we look briefly at a single underdeveloped country and review its efforts, supplemented by aid from abroad, to lift the burden of misery from its people. Almost any country in Asia, Africa, the Middle East, or Latin America would do, but India, with its nearly half-billion people, offers an especially moving and instructive example. Since its drive to raise living standards without violating basic human rights is in sharp contrast with the regimented, slavish approach to economic development in neighboring Red China, all the underdeveloped countries of Asia are carefully watching the outcome.

Five years after gaining independence in 1947, the government of India, with aid from the United States, the World Bank, and an international consortium, launched a 25-year economic-development program. The aim was to double the national income by 1977.

At the end of the first decade, despite backbreaking obstacles, considerable progress had been made. National income was up 40 percent. The rise in per-capita income, because of a 21.5 percent growth in population, was less striking, but even so it increased 17 percent. Output of mines and factories soared 70 percent. Though not coming up to expectations, food production increased 33 percent — a gain that was realized partly because an additional 20 million parched acres were brought under irrigation. The construction of dams more than doubled power-generating capacity, though a critical power shortage continued to exist and hinder progress.

These economic gains were matched by advances in health and education. Indians born in 1950 had an average life expectancy of 32 years. Ten years later, it was 42 years. Malaria is scarcely a problem any longer. As late as 1953, there were 75 million cases annually, and every year a million deaths were attributed to this debilitating disease. In recent years, the number of malaria cases has dropped to 100,000 a year. There has been improvement in health facilities generally, including an increase of 50 percent in hospital beds. Every year India's 72 medical schools are now graduating 4000 doctors.

In education, India had to start almost from scratch. In 1947, despite the efforts of missionaries and other private groups, the country was 80 percent illiterate. The illiteracy rate is still high, but India is gradually moving toward the constitutional goal of free, compulsory education for all children through age 14. By 1965, the government hopes to provide free schools for all children under 11. During the first decade of the development plan, primary education was extended to an additional 20 million children, so that school attendance just about doubled. Six of every ten children in the primary age group are now in school. There has also been some progress in secondary and higher education. India today has 37 universities and about 1250 colleges.

All this makes an inspiring story. But India's progress must be kept in perspective. As was said above, the aim of the 25-year program is to double the national income by 1977. If everything proceeds as planned — and already Red Chinese aggression in the fall of 1962 has caused distortions — per-capita income will eventually reach the pitiful figure of $100 a year. (By comparison, per-capita income in the United States was $2,366 in 1962).

A recent American traveler to India described his impressions of the country in this way:

India is a country today beset with troubles: indescribable poverty, food shortage, doctor shortage, housing shortage, school and teacher shortage, illiteracy, disease, unemployment, overcrowding and a rapidly expanding population.

With only a few changes here and there, that description fits all the underdeveloped countries in the world today. Practically without exception, they don't raise enough food, or enough of the right foods, to give their people a healthy diet. On the other hand, their populations are increasing much faster than the populations of the developed countries. At the present time, there is one European for every two Asians. If the postwar trend continues, by the year 2000 there will be only one European for every four Asians.

Demographers are agreed that population growth in the underdeveloped lands is not due to an increase in birthrates. Though their birthrates continue to be relatively high — 2 to 3 percent compared with 0.7 percent in Europe — it is the drop in death rates that mostly accounts for the additional mouths to feed. Improved medical care and hygiene, combined with long periods of peace, have destroyed the equilibrium between population and food supply that was formerly maintained by high infant mortality, epidemics, and war.

IV

One of the keys, then, to the development of poor nations lies in agriculture — in better methods, in improved seeds, in large increases in the use of fertilizer. There is more than a kernel of truth in the quip of an anonymous commentator that India is "not overpopulated, but underfertilized." Right now, the main trouble is that, despite help from the United Nations, the United States, and other countries, food production in the poor lands is not advancing fast enough. Actually, the imbalance between the rich and poor countries in agricultural output is greater today than it was before World War II. It is the rich countries that have profited most from the application of chemistry and technology to farming. In 1959, the UN Food and Agricultural Organization hopefully reported that world farm production in 1958–1959 increased more than twice as fast as population — 4 percent for farm output, 1.4 percent for population — but it was obliged to note that most of the gain in food production took place in the developed countries. That helps to explain why Latin America, the Far East, the Near East, and Africa, with three fifths of the world's population of three billion, account for only a third of total agricultural production.

The problem confronting the underdeveloped countries is enormous but, despite the pessimists, not insoluble. There is a sound basis for Pope John's reliance on the ability of man "to deepen and extend his mastery over nature." Truly, "the progress of science and technology achieved to date," as he said in *Mater et Magistra*, "opens up limitless horizons" (n. 189). Not so long ago, agricultural yields in India and Japan were about the same. Today, yields in Japan are three or four times what they are in India. Generally speaking, yields of meat and milk per head of cattle are extraordinarily low in all the underdeveloped countries — in the Far East, only a tenth of European yields; in Africa, only a seventh. In India, where merely the milk from cows is used, the yield per cow is a scant 40 gallons a year. In the United States it is 495 gallons, and in Holland 790 gallons.

No one pretends that the problem of reducing the imbalance in agricultural productivity between rich and poor nations is not a most difficult one. People are not easily led to abandon ancient ways of doing things. Sometimes it is hard even to persuade them to change a demonstrably deficient diet. And in cases where they are prepared to change, they lack both the education and capital needed to shift to modern techniques. People living on the margin of subsistence don't have much left over to pay for schools, tractors, and fertilizer plants. And the same goes, of course, for the capital equipment needed for industrial growth.

V

That is where foreign aid comes in, not as the sole, or even the main, answer to the needs of developing countries, but as an indispensable supplement to the efforts they themselves are making.

Sometimes tax-burdened citizens of the rich countries wonder why the peoples of the poor countries don't tighten their belts and finance their own development. Instead of coming to us with outstretched palms, the complaint goes, why don't they export more of their products to the rich countries, and in this way pay for the imports they need?

Apart from the fact that questions like these must seem

heartless to poor people, whose belts are already deplorably tight, they assume: (1) that the underdeveloped countries are not already paying for most of their improvements and are not constantly striving to pay for more of them by boosting their exports, and (2) that foreign markets are prepared to take at good prices all that the underdeveloped countries can produce and sell.

Neither assumption happens to be true.

In many underdeveloped countries, aid from abroad provides a relatively small part of the total need for capital and foreign exchange. For instance, the third five-year segment of India's economic plan calls for total investment of $23.6 billion. Only a little more than $4.6 billion of this will come from outside sources, under various foreign-aid programs. Most of the $4.8 billion budgeted for Pakistan's second five-year plan, which began July 1, 1960, is being paid for by exports and the savings of the people. Only a small fraction of total investment in Latin America is financed by American taxpayers under the Alliance for Progress.

As for exports, the underdeveloped countries wish only that they could sell more of their products abroad and get a better price for them. Unfortunately, for some years now, the conditions and terms of foreign trade have been highly unfavorable to them. This is not the least of the complications with which statesmen in the rich countries are wrestling as they struggle today for a better balance in the world economy.

All the underdeveloped countries depend for foreign exchange mainly on exports of foodstuffs — sugar, coffee, cocoa, tropical fruits — and industrial raw materials. But world demand for some of these goods is declining. As they grow in affluence, nations, like individuals, spend smaller percentages of their incomes on life's necessities, including food, and higher percentages on conveniences and luxuries.

Furthermore, technological progress has resulted in many economies in the use of industrial raw materials. The shift from the hot-dipping to the electrolytic process in producing tinplate, for example, has cut the percentage of tin used from 1.6 to .25. To countries like Bolivia and Malaya, which are heavily dependent on tin exports, this is a cruel development.

More significant still, all kinds of synthetic substitutes for raw materials have been discovered and perfected and have come into widespread use. Every housewife is aware that silk has lost ground to nylon, and that plastics are doing many jobs that glass, wood, and leather used to do. The story of synthetic rubber is especially dramatic. Thirty years ago, man-made rubber was only a trickle in world markets. Today, world production of synthetic rubber exceeds output of natural rubber. In the United States, which is easily the largest rubber user, synthetic has captured the lucrative automobile tire market and is now making inroads in the heavy-duty truck and bus tire market. In the first half of 1963, synthetic rubber accounted for nearly three fourths of all rubber consumption in the United States. It has been estimated that were it not for the growth of synthetic products, imports of raw materials by the developed countries would have been 40 percent higher over the past decade than they were. The case of rubber makes this seem very plausible.

Not only has demand for foodstuffs and raw materials declined in the developed countries; so have market prices. Since the Korean War, prices of raw materials and foodstuffs have dropped 5 percent, whereas prices of manufactured articles, which poor countries must import, have increased by 23 percent. In the case of particular commodities, price declines have been so sharp that they have more than wiped out all the benefits of foreign aid. This happened, for instance, to Colombia in 1957, when a drop of 11 cents a pound in world coffee prices cost the country four times its share of U. S. aid. The competitive battle between natural and synthetic rubber has had a softening effect on all rubber prices. During the summer of 1963, natural rubber fell to its lowest price in nine years — a development that had serious repercussions on a number of underdeveloped countries. All told, between 1955 and 1961, the net inflow of capital to developing countries, which amounted to $8 billion, barely compensated for their losses in foreign trade due to price deterioration. To the poor countries, it must seem at times as if foreign aid is only a partial return of the gains that rich countries are making from the terms of international trade.

A number of efforts have been made in the past, and continue to be made today, to control production and stabilize world prices of foodstuffs and raw materials. Some of these international commodity agreements, which aim at being fair to both producers and consumers, have been successful, but many have not. There appears to be growing agreement among the United States, Great Britain, and the Common Market countries of Western Europe that renewed attempts must be made, not only to assure stable prices for the exports of underdeveloped countries, but to increase demand for them among their peoples.

It is hard to see how the imbalances between rich and poor countries can ever be lessened unless progress is made in this difficult field. Not long ago, a group of experts at the United Nations estimated that if the economies of the underdeveloped countries expanded at the rate of 3 percent a year, their imports would have to jump from about $23 billion annually today to approximately $60 billion in 1980. The experts thought that by that time exports of manufactured goods, such as cotton textiles, might pay for as much as 25 percent of the bill for imports. For the rest of it, however, the underdeveloped countries would have to rely on traditional exports of raw materials and foodstuffs. The problem is certain to be extremely acute for the 25 or more underdeveloped countries that rely on a single commodity for half of their exports.

These figures indicate that foreign economic aid will have to continue for a long time to come. The burden on the United States may become lighter, however, as the years go on. Indeed, the burden is already lighter than it was fifteen years ago. At the beginning of the Marshall Plan, foreign economic and military aid was 2 percent of our gross national product, and 11.5 percent of the federal budget. In 1963, it was only seven tenths of 1 percent of the GNP and no more than 4.1 per cent of the budget. Meanwhile, some of the countries we helped after World War II are now sharing the burden of foreign aid with us. In 1956, Japan and Western Europe contributed $1.2 billion to underdeveloped countries. By 1962, they had doubled their aid. Three or four countries are currently devoting a larger percentage of their GNP to foreign aid than we are. Although some countries ought to do more than they are doing, the American contribution to reducing the economic disparities in the world is not out of proportion to our vast resources. This is not as clearly understood in the country as it ought to be.

VI

Finally, a word must be said about the population problem, since it is impossible to deal with imbalances in the world without noting it.

In modern times there has occurred something like a population explosion. From 1650, it took 200 years for the world's population to double. From 1850, it took just half that time. During the first half of the twentieth century, world population grew 60 percent. Some demographers estimate that it will double in the second half of the century. That would mean six billion people on the face of the earth in the year 2000. A 1958 UN report, *The Future Growth of World Population*, notes that whereas "it took 200,000 years for the world's human population to reach 2,500 million, it will now take a mere thirty years to add another 2,000 million." And so the story goes.

Discussing the pressure of population growth on natural resources in *Mater et Magistra*, Pope John describes with scholarly objectivity the fears of certain demographers:

Looking at the question on a world-wide scale, some consider that, according to sufficiently reliable statistics, the human race, in a few decades, will experience a notable increase in number, while the rate of economic growth will be considerably slower. Some take this to mean that unless something is done to check population growth, the lack of balance between size of population and the means of subsistence will make itself felt more acutely in the not too distant future (n. 186).

Continuing in a similarly objective vein, the Pope notes apprehensions about the special problem of the underdeveloped countries:

It is clear that in the less-developed nations — still relying on statistical data — the rapid spread of modern hygienic methods and medical remedies reduces the death rate among infants, and thus lengthens the life-span. At the same time, the number of births, where it is now normally high, tends to remain more or less constant, at least for a considerable period of time. But while the number of births exceeds the number of deaths in the same year, the productive efficiency of the respective economic systems does not increase proportionately. Accordingly, an improvement in the standard of living in these under-developed states is almost impossible. Indeed, it is rather inevitable that things will get worse. Hence, to avoid a situation which will result in extreme hardship, there are those who would have recourse to drastic measures of birth control or birth prevention (n. 187).

While conceding that the population problem is serious "in certain underdeveloped areas and states," Pope John rejects the overall appraisal of the pessimistic school of demographers. "The truth is," he writes, "that the relation between the size of the world population and the available world resources does not seem — at least for the moment and in the near future — to create a serious difficulty" (n. 188).

He felt that there were too many uncertainties in the present situation and too much controversy about future trends to warrant hard and fast conclusions at this time.

It is certainly true that the history of population projections is not such as to warrant an act of faith in the prophetic capacities of demographers. Furthermore, the concept itself of overpopulation is a very slippery one. There does not appear to be a necessary relationship between population and cultivable land. No part of the world is more densely populated than Western Europe, yet Europe as a whole enjoys one of the highest living standards in the world. On the other hand, Africa, which is the least densely populated of all the continents, has the world's lowest living standard. Few countries are more densely populated than Holland, yet the Dutch, who are a well-fed people, export 40 percent of their agricultural production. Although it is obvious that much of the earth's surface cannot be cultivated, it is hard to believe that if the incentive were present, men could not find ways of bringing under the plow considerably more than the 9 or 10 percent of the world's land surface that we are presently cultivating.

Pope John does not minimize the population problem. He insists only that it must not be solved by means that degrade human beings and are contrary to God's law. The answer is to be found, he stresses, "only in socio-economic progress achieved in a moral atmosphere befitting the dignity of mankind and the immense value of a single human life" (n. 192). His trust in God goes hand in hand with great confidence in man:

> God in His goodness and wisdom has implanted in nature inexhaustible resources and has endowed man with a sufficient measure of intelligence to create instruments fit to turn its products to the satisfaction of his needs and wants (n. 189).

Those who are familiar with the marvelous progress that has already been made in increasing agricultural yields and in bringing under cultivation lands that were formerly considered hopelessly barren will understand that the Pope is not giving utterance to merely pious hopes and fancies.

As for those underdeveloped countries which do have a serious population problem, we can talk of the pressure of population on resources only in a qualified sense. So long as some countries in the world feel obliged, as does the United States, to pursue a restrictionist farm policy, so long as people and foodstuffs, capital and technical aid are unable to flow freely between countries, we cannot in logic and justice argue that the natural resources which God created to sustain the whole human race are inadequate for their purpose. The failure today, and the threatened failure tomorrow, are of human origin, not divine.

CHAPTER 11

Toward a Just Social Order

In light of the social implications of Christian belief, what moral judgment should be passed on our American capitalistic system?

Over a large part of the world, and especially in Latin America, capitalism is severely criticized and often condemned on moral grounds. On May 1, 1963, for instance, the National Council of Bishops of Brazil issued a statement demanding radical changes in the economic system of their country. The reason they gave for reform was this:

> Ours is an order still vitiated by the heavy weight of the capitalist tradition that dominated the West in past centuries. It is an order of things in which economic power (money) still maintains the last word in regard to economic, political and social decisions. It is an order in which the minority people with means have every door open to culture, to higher levels of living in regard to health, comfort and luxury, while the majority, those without means, are in the very nature of things deprived of the exercise of many of the fundamental rights mentioned in *Pacem in Terris*.

No one can suppose, the Brazilian hierarchy concludes, that "such an order of things is a Christian order."

How are we to estimate anticapitalist statements of this kind?

For Catholics, the problem has been made more difficult because of certain references to capitalism in the addresses of Pope Pius XII. Some foreign critics have interpreted these as condemnatory of our system of private enterprise. Are these critics reading the mind of Pius XII correctly? Let us see.

I

The case against capitalism derived from the teaching of Pius XII stands or falls on three passages from his collected addresses.

Setting forth the Christian concept of property in a radio address on September 1, 1944, Pius XII rejected a social order in which the "natural right to property is denied in principle or nullified in practice." He went on to say, as we already saw in Chapter 3, that the Christian conscience is also unable to accept a concept of private property that is opposed to a true social order.

> Accordingly, where, for instance, "capitalism" is based on such false concepts and arrogates to itself an unlimited right over property, without any subordination to the common good, the Church has condemned it as contrary to natural law.

Pope Pius mentioned capitalism again in an allocution on October 21, 1945, to a large group of Catholic women:

> On the other hand, can a woman hope for her real well-being from a regime dominated by capitalism? We do not need to describe to you now the economic and social results that issue from it. You know its characteristic signs, and you yourselves are bearing its burden: excessive concentration of populations in cities, the constant all-absorbing increase of big businesses, the difficult and precarious state of other, especially small, producers employing craftsmen, and even more of agriculture, and the disturbing increase of unemployment.

Finally, in an apostolic exhortation to the clergy on September 23, 1950 — Menti Nostrae — the Pope criticized priests "who show themselves fearful and uncertain when faced with the wickedness of communism," as well as those who are "no less timid and uncertain in the face of that economic system which is known as capitalism, the grave consequences of which the Church has not failed to denounce."

In considering these texts, which on the surface appear to condemn capitalistic systems, one must bear in mind that the papacy is nothing if not consistent. We must assume that Pope Pius XII wished to affirm and develop the teachings of his predecessors, not to contradict them. Indeed, he pointedly referred on a number of occasions to the social encyclicals of Leo XIII and Pius XI.

The first thing to note about those encyclicals is that the word "capitalism" rarely occurs. Why their authors avoided a terminology that seems natural to us, we do not know. It is possible, however, to suggest two plausible reasons.

One is that the Popes wished to avoid any identification of their criticism of the contemporary economic order with the strictures of Karl Marx. This might have led the unwary to believe — despite the clear papal condemnation of Marxist socialism — that the founder of communism and the heads of the Catholic Church were saying much the same thing and, by inference, advocating similar remedies and solutions.

In the second place, both Leo XIII and Pius XI must have been aware of the lack of precision in the meaning and usage of the word "capitalism." To this day it suffers from ambiguity. In addition, it is so heavily charged with emotional overtones — many of them the result of Marxist propaganda — that it lends itself more readily to the designs of the demagogue than to the religious teacher.

At any rate, Leo XIII did not once use the word "capitalism" in Rerum Novarum, and Pius XI resorted to it sparingly. As we have already seen, what Leo condemned as incompatible with the natural law, he called "economic individualism" or "economic liberalism" — terms that can be precisely defined, and which have the added merit of historical justification. Pope Pius XI followed the example of Leo, and there is not the slightest reason to believe that Pope Pius XII, despite a handful of references to capitalism, wished to abandon their terminology. Those who want to show, therefore, that Pius XII condemned American capitalism must demonstrate that American capitalism and economic liberalism, or economic individualism, are identical. For it is clear from the context that when Pius

XII uses *"capitalism"* he means *"economic liberalism."*

Consider his use of the word in the radio address of September 1, 1944. By stating that the Church has condemned capitalism *where it is based on a false concept of private property,* the Pope plainly indicates that there are different kinds of capitalistic systems, and that where a capitalistic system is not based on a false concept of property the Church does not condemn it. He carefully explains this erroneous concept. It is one that regards the right of private property as unlimited and absolute, with no recognition of its social aspects, or of the necessity of subordinating its exercise to the demands of the common good. But that is precisely the concept of private property that is characteristic of economic liberalism. Pius XII is only reaffirming Leo's rejection of laissez faire.

Similarly in *Menti Nostrae,* the Pope is condemning capitalism in a qualified sense. Though that is sufficiently evident from the text itself — he is rejecting a system which "the Church has never ceased to denounce," i.e., economic liberalism — there is a more compelling reason for this interpretation. The English text of *Menti Nostrae* cited above is a translation of the Italian version of the exhortation. A literal translation from the official Latin text reads as follows:

> Others show themselves no less timid and uncertain in the face of that economic system which derives its name from the excessive massing of private wealth, the serious effects of which the Church has never ceased to denounce.

Thus the word "capitalism," which occurs in the Italian, does not appear in the original Latin. On being asked to clarify the meaning of the phrase, "that economic system which derives its name from the excessive amassing of private wealth," Antonio Cardinal Bacci, secretary of the Vatican Secretariate for Briefs to Princes, replied: "Excessive or exaggerated capitalism." In the context of papal social teaching, this can only mean that kind of capitalism which ignores or denies the social obligations of ownership and is, as a consequence, properly known as economic liberalism or individualism.

In the address to women, Pope Pius mentions certain features of contemporary economic life that are disadvantageous to women — excessive urbanization, unemployment, unrestrained growth of big business, precarious position of agriculture and small business. All these developments are abuses of a system in which, as Pope Pius XI said, "some provide capital while others provide labor for a joint economic activity" (QA, n. 100). They are certainly not necessary and inevitable results of the system, since they are not everywhere present today, and, where they are present, are not verified in the same degree. On the face of it, Pius XII was talking about the contemporary economic system, popularly known as capitalism, in the same way in which Pius XI wrote about it in *Quadragesimo Anno*:

> With all his energy, Leo XIII sought to adjust this economic system according to the norms of right order; hence, it is evident that this system is not to be condemned in itself. And surely it is not of its own nature vicious (n. 101).

We are left, then, with the key question: Is the American system of private enterprise identical with economic liberalism, which the papacy has certainly condemned?

Whatever doubts one might have had fifty years or more ago, there can be little question today about the basic moral soundness of the American system of private enterprise. Those who confuse it with the laissez-faire capitalism of the nineteenth century are ignoring a half century of constructive change and development.

There is today in the United States no unrestricted right to the use of private property. That right has been legally circumscribed in numerous ways on both the federal and state level. Factory inspection laws, wage-and-hour legislation, prohibition of child labor, special protection of women workers, rules on corporate financing, building codes, curbs on advertising, pure food and drug laws, ordinances against consumer frauds — in these and many other ways public authority has prescribed, in the words of Pope Pius XI, "what is and is not permitted to owners in the use of their property" (QA, n. 49). Furthermore, a number of industries closely connected with the common good — all forms of public transportation, radio and television, telephone and telegraph, gas and electricity — are regulated by federal or local agencies. As a result, private owners are obliged to have some regard for the general welfare, whether they wish to or not, and to treat their employees as something more than so many items in the cost of production. Finally, excessive individualism has also been significantly curbed by the legal protection afforded the right of workers to organize and bargain collectively.

In short, all the freedoms vindicated by economic liberalism — freedom of trade and freedom of contract, freedom from interference by government or private groups — have been sharply curtailed in the United States. Although some businessmen still talk the language of economic individualism, a growing number of them, especially by their emphasis on the social responsibilities of industry and their willingness to deal honorably with trade unions, are abandoning the slogans as well as the practice of laissez-faire capitalism.

If we measure the American system in terms of the rights of man as set forth by Pope John in the opening chapters of *Pacem in Terris*, we can also find reasons for modest satisfaction. Most Americans have the means "necessary and suitable for the proper development of life" (n. 11). They have food, clothing, shelter, recreational opportunity, and the best medical care available anywhere. Through either government or private insurance programs, or through public assistance, or as a result of benefits connected with employment, they have security in case of sickness, inability to work, widowhood, old age, unemployment, and in other cases in which, through no fault of their own, they lack the means of subsistence. They also enjoy the economic rights the Pope enumerates: free initiative, job opportunities, safe conditions of work, ownership and fair wages. Not many economic systems in the world — if any at all — provide a more substantial material basis for personal and family development than ours does, or are more in accord with human dignity.

That is not the same thing as saying that the American system of private enterprise and the society to which it has given a special tone are ready for baptism. By no means. As Pope Pius XII said in a broader context, the Church "does not intend to defend absolutely and simply the present state of affairs as if she saw in it the expression of God's will . . ." (Address on September 1, 1944). Although many Americans have ample reason to be satisfied with the *status quo*, many others do not. There are gross injustices in American life, and many unsolved problems. If God-fearing men were to rest content with things as they are, the full promise of America would never be achieved. The great struggle for a society dedicated to justice and freedom, to truth and love is only half won. We may not be able to see as yet all the challenges ahead, but enough of them are already sufficiently evident and pressing to keep us busy for a long time to come.

II

There is the scandalously unfinished business of our colored citizens. Their housing, which is frequently restricted to segregated neighborhoods, is by and large grossly substandard. Their jobless rate is consistently higher than that of whites (Negroes are the last hired, the first fired). When they do work, they are mostly employed in menial and low-paying jobs. As a consequence, although Negroes are 11 percent of the population, they receive only 5 percent of personal income. In 1962, according to the Southern Regional Council, about 60 percent of Negro families made less than $4,000 a year. Nearly 45 percent made less than $3,000 a year. Only slowly, as we saw in Chapter 8, are old barriers against the admission of Negroes to managerial positions and to membership in craft unions being broken down. By and large, Negro children are deprived of the educational opportunities that most white children enjoy. In many Southern states, the right of our colored citizens to vote — to use their political power to abolish the injustices from which they suffer — is callously abridged. In numerous irritating and demeaning ways, they are treated as second-class citizens.

On the matter of interracial relations, Catholics can scarcely plead ignorance as an excuse for unjust words and actions. In the midst of World War II, when our white and colored soldiers were dying side by side in Europe and Asia, the American bishops wrote of American Negroes as follows:

> We owe to these fellow citizens, who have contributed so largely to the development of our country, and for whose welfare history imposes on us a special obligation of justice, to see that they have in fact the rights which are given them in our Constitution. This means not only political equality, but also fair economic and educational opportunities, a just share in public welfare projects, good housing without exploitation, and a full chance for the social advancement of their race (Annual Statement, November 11, 1943).

Fifteen years later, as white opposition to Negro demands for justice grew, the bishops returned to the subject. In their annual statement on November 13, 1958, they said:

> Discrimination based on the accidental fact of race or color, and as such injurious to human rights regardless of personal qualities or achievements, cannot be reconciled with the truth that God has created all men with equal rights and equal dignity.

After quoting the statement made by Pope Pius XII (on September 7, 1956), "God did not create a human family made up of segregated, dissociated, mutually independent members," the bishops continued:

> It is a matter of historical fact that segregation in our country has led to oppressive conditions and the denial of basic human rights for the Negro. This is evident in the fundamental fields of education, job opportunity and housing.

Finally, the bishops prayed that "responsible and sober-minded Americans of all religious faiths, in all areas of our land," would seize "the mantle of leadership from the agitator and the racist." They added: "It is vital that we act now and act decisively."

If after these clear statements by the American hierarchy any Catholic still doubts that the race question is basically moral and religious, let him read *Pacem in Terris*. In that encyclical Pope John settled the matter once and for all time when he said bluntly that "doctrinally racial discrimination can in no way be justified" (n. 44).

III

The high unemployment rate among Negroes adds poignancy to a postwar development that is rightly worrying many Americans. Despite tangible progress in several directions, as we saw in Chapter 8, the economy has been unable to provide jobs for all those able and willing to work. Even the figures given there do not tell the whole disturbing story. While total employment reached 67.8 million in 1962, many of the new jobs did not represent full-time work. Between 1953 and 1962, the number of part-time workers jumped from 8.6 million to 11.7 million. Many of these part-time workers were Negroes. In fact, of all Negroes employed in nonfarm jobs in 1962, 10 percent worked only part-time.

Furthermore, since the expansion in employment was confined to the service industries, such as retail and wholesale trade, transportation and public utilities, finance, insurance and real estate, and government on all levels, the outlook for unskilled and semiskilled workers became bleaker than ever. It is unfortunately true that wages for the only kind of work they are qualified to perform are generally lower in the service industries than they are in the goods-producing industries. Among other things, this means that young people who drop out of school or fail to acquire a skill of some kind face a hard economic future.

In the national debate now in progress over policies for

lowering the stubbornly high jobless level, some economists stress the need of educating and training workers, while others emphasize faster economic growth. The former consider today's unemployment primarily "structural" — the result, that is, of swift technological change. The latter regard it as dominantly "cyclical" — the consequence of the failure of the economy to rebound vigorously enough from postwar recessions.

These positions do not appear to be irreconcilable. Those who identify "automation" as the main cause of unemployment willingly grant that a faster rate of economic growth would make it much easier than it would otherwise be to find jobs for technologically displaced workers. In the same way, those who emphasize economic growth would probably agree that without retraining and help in moving from depressed areas many of today's unemployed would remain jobless even in the midst of a boom.

Meanwhile, there is a growing movement for a reduction in hours of work. Over the years, as the process of mechanization went on, the length of the workday and workweek has steadily shortened. A century ago, male workers in New England textile mills had a 12-hour day and a 72-hour week. By the end of the nineteenth century, the 10-hour day and 60-hour week had become fairly common. In 1914, Henry Ford, to the consternation of many fellow employers, introduced the 8-hour day in manufacturing. Although industry in general continued to resist shorter hours, arguing that a workweek shorter than 50 or 54 hours was impractical, the 40-hour week began to appear in the 1920's. It is now a quarter century since the Fair Labor Standards Act made the 40-hour week more or less standard in all businesses involved in interstate commerce. Naturally, a good many people are now asking, in view of the technological progress made since 1938, whether the time has not come for another reduction in working hours.

In fact, for some years now, a reduction of working hours has been quietly taking place as a result of collective bargaining and of competition for office workers. In many offices and in some industries, the 35-hour or 37-hour week has become normal practice. In other industries, paid holidays and vacations with pay have been notably extended. We have already seen that the basic steel industry recently granted a 13-week paid vacation every five years to half the workers covered by its contracts with the United Steelworkers of America.

Those who advocate a reduction in working hours hope that this will multiply job openings. This hope could be frustrated, at least in part, if employers chose to schedule more overtime, or if workers already employed took on a second job. It would be frustrated, too, if many women not now in the labor market were tempted by shorter work days to leave their homes for part-time jobs.

Although the cause of our high jobless rate and the remedies for dealing with it may be controversial matters, there is wide agreement that the evil cannot be tolerated. As Pope John taught in *Pacem in Terris*, human beings have a natural right to work (cf. n. 18). This is one of the most basic and necessary of all rights, and no economic society can pass moral muster until it succeeds in guaranteeing it.

IV

In *Quadragesimo Anno*, Pope Pius XI underlined a suicidal tendency inherent in laissez-faire capitalism. Referring to the concentration of immense economic power in the hands of a few, "who often are not the owners but only the trustees and managing directors of invested funds," the Pope said that this development "is the fruit that the unlimited freedom of struggle among competitors has of its own nature produced. . . . Free competition has destroyed itself; economic dictatorship has supplanted the free market" (nn. 105–109).

Although we have long been aware of this problem in the United States, we have not yet found a satisfactory answer to it. Reacting to the growth of trusts and monopolies in the post-Civil War period, Congress passed the Sherman Antitrust Act in 1890. In an effort to preserve competition as the regulator of the economy, it declared:

> 1. Every contract, combination in the form of trust or otherwise, or conspiracy in restraint of trade or commerce among the several States, or with foreign nations, is . . . hereby declared to be illegal.
> 2. Every person who shall monopolize, or attempt to monopolize . . . any part of the trade or commerce among the several States, or with foreign nations, shall be deemed guilty of a misdemeanor.

The law provided various penalties for infractions, including fines, imprisonment, dissolution of monopolistic corporations and suits for triple damages.

Despite additional efforts by Congress over the years to close loopholes in the Sherman Act, including the Clayton Act of 1914, the tendency toward huge concentrations of economic power in key markets has continued almost without interruption. Violations of the law have been numerous and there is scarcely a large blue-chip corporation in the country that has not run afoul of the Antitrust Division of the U. S. Department of Justice. In the business community, a conviction for offenses under the antitrust laws carries no stigma at all. When several years ago a federal judge sentenced seven executives to jail for engaging in a price-fixing conspiracy in the electrical equipment industry, there was a widespread feeling in business circles that he had broken the unwritten rules of the game. The rules called, traditionally, for no more than a gentle monetary slap on the wrist.

Something must be wrong with a law that is so frequently violated by men who loudly profess a belief in a system of competitive enterprise.

One school of thought maintains that the Sherman Act incorporates a contradiction, and that, as a consequence, it is impossible in some cases to obey it without defeating its purpose. Section I of the law forbids conspiracy in restraint of trade and commerce. Section II prohibits monopoly or any "attempt to monopolize . . . any part of the trade or commerce among the several States. . . ." In certain industries, this school argues, the only way the strongest company, or companies, can avoid monopolization is by engaging in a conspiracy to control prices and allocate markets. If they do not do this, if instead they compete vigorously, they will force the smaller and less efficient producers in the industry into bankruptcy and thus risk the charge of seeking to establish a monopoly. This situation is said to exist in practically all the major cyclical industries — steel, machinery, electrical equipment, textiles.

The charge has also been made that the Sherman Act is simply out of date. It envisaged markets in which many producers competed for the custom of many buyers and the price was determined by a free interplay of forces. In most cases, such markets do not exist, and have not existed for a long time. Underlying most business conduct today — and government policy as well — is a conviction that a limit exists beyond which price fluctuations become socially intolerable and must be avoided. In practice, price fluctuations are controlled by the price leadership of a dominant corporation, or by informal, unwritten agreements among competitors. Over large areas of industry, "administered" prices have replaced "competitive" prices. Consequently, some authorities contend that the antitrust laws should be revised to reflect contemporary realities.

Finally, still another school of thought remains firm in the belief that the competitive ideal of the Sherman Act can still be largely realized despite the concentration that has already occurred. The tide, these thinkers believe, can be reversed by tough enforcement of the law and by strenuous attempts to break up many of the nation's huge corporations. They are persuaded that the only alternative to this policy is constantly increasing public control of big business or, perhaps, even public ownership.

One of the difficulties of formulating an antitrust policy

is the ambivalent attitude of the American people.

On the one hand, Americans are still attracted to the Jeffersonian vision of a nation of small, independent, enterprising farmers and businessmen. No one aspiring to office in this country would think of depreciating the little, self-reliant enterpriser, or of suggesting that he is anything but the salt of the American earth. It is no accident that both Houses of Congress have a standing Small Business Committee. Remnants of the old suspicion of Wall Street and the trusts remain, and the public-relations people in industry must constantly reckon with this.

On the other hand, Americans are proud of our big corporations. They buy their stock, purchase their products, watch their television shows. More often than not they are eager and happy to work for them. To many people, General Motors, Standard Oil of New Jersey, and the Atlantic and Pacific Tea Company are just as American as are the local family-owned machine shop, the independent filling station, and the corner grocery store. So long as this outlook prevails in its present unsophisticated form, with no distinction made between bigness dictated by capital, technological, or other requirements, and bigness that is not so dictated, no new approach to the antitrust laws is likely to be attempted.

From the viewpoint of the Church's social teaching, the ideal would be a competitive system functioning under rules that keep the market struggle within socially tolerable bounds. These rules would necessarily have to define "fair" competition, using as a yardstick the virtues of justice and charity. That is what Pope Pius XI seems to be recommending in the paragraphs cited above. By and large, scholars inspired by Christian social principles have not given this whole subject anything like the attention it deserves.

Meanwhile, we have no choice for the present but to encourage small business, by legislation if necessary, and to maintain a close supervision over the operations of big business. In *Mater et Magistra*, Pope John makes his own a recommendation of Pope Pius XII that "small and average-size undertakings in agriculture, in the arts and crafts, in commerce and industry, should be safeguarded and fostered by allowing them to share in the advantages of larger firms through entry into co-operative unions" (n. 84). With respect to big business, the Pope teaches that government has the duty "to make certain that the aims pursued by the directors of leading companies, especially those having the greatest impact on the national economy, are not contrary to the demands of the common good" (n. 104).

V

Bigness in business, together with the modern revolution in technology, transport, and communications, has led to bigness in other fields — in government, in labor, in agriculture, and in the professions. American socioeconomic life has become highly organized into a bewildering multiplicity of occupational groups — trade associations, chambers of commerce, medical and legal societies, educational associations, farm organizations, and trade unions. As Pope John says in *Mater et Magistra*, "today almost nobody hears, much less pays attention to, isolated voices" (n. 146).

This evolution of group life has aroused fears that individual men, who "are of necessity the foundation, the cause and the reason for the existence of all social institutions" (MM, n. 219), are losing their freedom to grow and perfect themselves as persons. They are becoming, in a fashionable phrase, "organization men," with no independent life of their own. Accordingly, it is said, the whole purpose of economic activity — to furnish the material basis for a truly human life — is being frustrated by the mechanization of contemporary culture.

In dealing with the phenomenon of socialization — understood in the sense of an organized or group approach to problems and challenges in contemporary society — Pope John draws up a balance sheet. On the one side, he lists its many advantages, all of them deriving from the fact that "patterns of group life" and juridically established "social institutions" make possible "the satisfaction of many personal rights." On the other side, he enumerates possible disadvantages, all of which proceed from the danger that socialization may restrict the individual's freedom and hamper the development of his personality (cf. nn. 61–62).

Is socialization, then, an obstacle and threat to human progress? Does it destroy the individual, absorb him into an impersonal mass, turn him into an automaton?

By no means, Pope John concludes. Socialization is not the product of blind, mechanical forces working in a deterministic way. Rather it is the result of the free actions of human beings who by nature are disposed to act in a responsible manner. Admittedly, the growing interdependence of men in modern society and other environmental elements do exert pressure on men to organize; but, then, it is natural for men to collaborate with others, to pool resources in order to attain objectives that are beyond their individual reach. It is possible, therefore, to develop an organic society in such a manner that the advantages of socialization are enhanced and its disadvantages minimized (cf. nn. 62–65).

If prudent procedures are followed, the Pope continues, the network of organizations in contemporary life, both public and private, will not seriously restrict individuals but will offer them instead opportunities for self-expression and personal development (cf. n. 67).

Whether or not socialization evolves in a human, constructive way depends, the Pope says, on the fulfillment of a number of conditions. It depends on the ability of governments to know when their intervention is needed and when it is not. It depends on a grant of freedom and independence to nongovernmental organizations. It depends on the moral capacity of these private groups to pursue their objectives without injury to the common good. It depends, finally, on their democratic character (cf. n. 65).

In this country, with its individualistic traditions, nongovernmental groups are free to conduct their affairs with a minimum of interference from public authorities. The danger among us is that in pursuing their goals private societies frequently lack a broad enough social perspective. Too often they act as mere pressure groups — frequently in competition with other groups — under the assumption that what is good for them is also good for the country. The pursuit of group interests in rivalry with other groups is not bad in itself. In fact it often leads in a democratic society to tolerable compromises and workable public policies. But power struggles of this kind can be dangerous. If the conflict is pushed to extremes, the meat of one group becomes the poison of others, with the result that no room is left for accommodation and compromise. A more conscious appreciation of the general welfare, together with a heightened respect for the rights of others, would tend to moderate demands and keep self-interest within socially acceptable bounds.

In countries that lack a democratic tradition and have a low educational level, one might expect that private organizations would be administered on authoritarian lines. In well-established democracies, the heavy-handed dictator should be the exception. In this country the danger from within to healthy group life comes in most cases, as we would expect, not from dictatorial leaders, but from apathetic members. Americans are notorious joiners. They are equally notorious for their willingness "to let George do it." It has often been remarked that the American male, once the day's work is done, is so attracted to the comforts of his home that he has to be almost literally dragged from it to attend meetings. Some trade unions, intent on developing democratic participation in their affairs, have experimented with money fines for nonattendance, but even this pocketbook pressure is not always successful. It is unfortunately true that many Americans are more sensitive to the rights of membership than its duties.

The apathy of members places a great strain, of course, on the integrity of leaders, and the surprising thing is not that scandals have occurred in trade unions and other organizations, but that they have not occurred more frequently.

It is sometimes said that the issues with which an organization must deal are so complicated and technical nowadays that the average member cannot be expected to understand them. Though there is much validity in that observation, it cannot be offered as an excuse for irresponsible membership. Just as men in their capacity of citizens must make an effort to understand public issues and cast an informed vote, so they are obliged to participate as intelligently and responsibly as they can in the affairs of their organizations. This obligation increases in gravity in direct proportion to the importance of the organization.

As the result of the growing complexity of life, our larger nongovernmental organizations are often obliged to develop bureaucracies and turn over to them a large area of administration. Increasingly, elected officials are becoming more and more dependent on the specialized knowledge of hired assistants. Indeed, officials can scarcely chart an intelligent and practical policy without their professional help. This places a great premium on the development of men and women of high character and intelligence who are willing to devote their talents to the well-being of organizations. The economist for a trade union, the lawyer for a trade association, the legislative representative for a farm group — all perform a function that is scarcely less necessary to a just and smooth-working society than is the function of the public servant in government. The vocation of a bureaucrat, in private as well as public bodies, is truly a noble one. It emphasizes service to one's fellowmen more directly than do many other callings in life. It should be ambitioned more often than it is.

All in all, socialization has contributed to progress toward social justice in American society. It has kept alive the spirit of self-help. In many ways it has bridged the gap between the individual citizen and his government. It must be perfected, however, along the lines mentioned by Pope John if it is to achieve its full promise and skirt the pitfalls in its way.

VI

In addition to racial discrimination, dearth of employment opportunities, concentration of economic power, organizational weaknesses, and other defects and evils noted in earlier chapters (especially maldistribution of wealth and income, and the glaring persistence of poverty in the midst of plenty), American economic society has been criticized for its materialism. By this is meant that the American people have a distorted sense of values, that they tend to equate happiness and success with material possessions, that they are insensitive to the finer things of life — to literature and the arts, to philosophy and religion.

To some extent, this criticism is justified, although it is not nearly so justified as foreigners sometimes imagine. Behind the materialistic façade of our affluent society, there are spiritual and cultural riches that often go unnoticed. Americans are not as bad as their flashy paperbacks often suggest that they are. We have our greedy hucksters, our racketeers, our vulgar nouveaux riches, but what society doesn't?

It would be foolish, however, to ignore the critics, and even more foolish to make little of the temptations that are inseparable from material and technological progress. Not that this progress is bad. On the contrary, as Pope John says in Mater et Magistra, "the Church has always taught and continues to teach that scientific and technical progress and the resultant material well-being are truly good and, as such, must be regarded as an important sign of progress in human civilization" (n. 246). Nevertheless, when men become deeply immersed in material pursuits, the danger is always present that they may forget the true purpose of life and adopt almost unconsciously a false hierarchy of values. This can the more easily happen in modern commercial societies where advertising has developed into a major industry. Some of the motives stressed by advertisers — pride, envy, love of luxury, sexual appeal — cannot readily be harmonized with the Christian ideal of life. We all need to keep before our minds the words of Jesus Christ: "For what does it profit a man if he gain the whole world and suffer the loss of his own soul?" (Mt 16:26.)

At the present time, a number of projects, public as well as private, are under way to raise the moral standards of industry, labor, and government. This is a very important development, since it is aimed directly at restoring the domination of morality over public life. This traditional domination was weakened, as we have seen, by the popular eighteenth-century idea of an autonomous marketplace, which led in turn to a lamentable moral separation between a man's private life and his life in business. Though the divorce never went as far in practice as the theory warranted, it did have the result of lowering ethical standards in public life.

The task of improving the moral climate of the marketplace necessarily requires a twofold approach, as we saw in Chapter 1. Changes are required in both economic institutions and in the hearts of men. On the one hand, unprincipled men can destroy the most perfect institutional framework ever devised; and, on the other, bad institutions make it extremely difficult, if not impossible, for good men to act uprightly and survive financially. Higher personal standards are essential, but so are enforceable codes of fair business practice. Without such codes to supplement existing laws against unjust conduct, men of goodwill often find themselves in situations where it is hard to know right from wrong. As Pope John says, what justice requires in some cases is not easy to determine (cf. MM, n. 229).

Societies cannot long remain on dead center, materially or spiritually. Either they progress or they decline. In today's harsh circumstances, we have an exceptionally strong motive to do everything possible to improve our economy and to raise its moral tone. However dismaying the fact may be, millions of people in the world, especially in the underdeveloped countries, are by no means persuaded that our capitalistic way of life is worth imitating. Many of them find in communism, not only more promising approaches to their own economic development, but also a greater concern for justice for all.

We may protest that these people have no understanding of communism, and we can strive to show them its fallacies in theory and its failures in practice. We can warn them that communism will destroy their ancient traditions, including their sacred religious practices. We can point out that communism and freedom are irreconcilable. In so doing, perhaps we can save some of them from Marxian slavery.

It is in none of these ways, however, that the communist threat to the world will be finally repelled. Words and arguments can help, but they will not be decisive. Only the power of example can win the terrible struggle for the soul of the modern world. "It is not enough merely to publicize a social doctrine," Pope John warns in *Mater et Magistra*. "It has to be translated into action." And "this is particularly true," he adds, "of Christian social doctrine, whose light is truth, whose objective is justice, and whose driving force is love" (n. 226). Unless our performance matches our beliefs, we cannot hope to give a "human and Christian tone to modern civilization" (n. 256). It is to this noble and enormous task that the Church, through its social teaching, summons Catholics and invites all men of goodwill.

Bibliographical Note

The chief sources of the Catholic Church's socioeconomic teaching are four papal encyclicals:

Rerum Novarum ("On the condition of Workers"), Leo XIII, 1891;

Quadragesimo Anno ("On Reconstructing the Social Order"), Pius XI, 1931;

Mater et Magistra ("Christianity and Social Progress"), John XXIII, 1961;

Pacem in Terris ("Peace on Earth"), John XXIII, 1963.

To this list should be added two other encyclicals of Pius XI: *Divini Redemptoris* ("On Atheistic Communism"), 1937; and *Casti Connubii* ("On Christian Marriage"), 1930.

All these titles are available from the Paulist Press. Large excerpts from them (except *Casti Connubii*) appear in Anne Fremantle's *The Social Teachings of the Church* (New American Library, 1963). The America Press has editions of *Mater et Magistra* and *Pacem in Terris* that include commentary, bibliography, and study-club outline. The America Press also offers a translation of *Casti Connubii* with study aids. *The Pope Speaks* publishes translations of *Mater et Magistra* and *Pacem in Terris*.

Though Pius XII wrote no socioeconomic encyclical, he treated social questions in many of his allocutions and radio addresses. Most of these were published in the *Catholic Mind* and are available in the bound volumes. Another handy source for Pope Pius XII is *The Pope Speaks*. Finally, many of the addresses appear in *Major Addresses of Pius XII*, ed. by Rev. Vincent A. Yzermans (North Central Publishing Co., 1961).

The American hierarchy has made a number of pronouncements on social questions. The chief ones are the following:

"Bishops' Program of Social Reconstruction," 1919;

"Statement on the Present Crisis," 1933;

"Christian Attitude on Social Problems," 1937;

"Church and Social Order," 1940;

"Discrimination and the Christian Conscience," 1958.

The statement on discrimination appeared in the *Catholic Mind*,

January–February, 1959. All the other statements are printed in *Our Bishops Speak*, Raphael M. Huber, O.F.M. Conv. (Bruce, 1952).

Among older books on the Church's social teaching, John A. Ryan's *Distributive Justice*, 3 ed. (Macmillan, 1942), Francis J. Haas's *Man and Society*, 2 ed. (Appleton-Century), Raymond J. Miller's *Forty Years After: Pius XI and the Social Order* (Radio Replies Press, 1947), and Mary Lois Eberdt and Gerald Schnepp's *Industrialism and the Popes* (Kenedy, 1952) have best weathered the passing of time. The Eberdt-Schnepp book is especially useful to those interested in labor-management cooperation. It has an extensive bibliography. Johannes Messner's *Social Ethics* (Herder, 1949) is recognized as a kind of classic in its field.

Among newer books, three are outstanding: *Social Principles and Economic Life*, Rev. John F. Cronin, S.S. (Bruce, 1959); *The Church and Social Justice*, Jean-Yves Calvez, S.J., and Jacques Perrin, S.J. (Regnery, 1961); and *The Functional Economy*, Bernard W. Dempsey, S.J. (Prentice-Hall, 1958). Father Cronin's booklet, *The Social Teaching of Pope John XXIII* (Bruce, 1963), complements his earlier work. Other recent studies are *Christianity and Economics*, Christopher Hollis (Hawthorn, 1961); *The Challenge of Mater et Magistra*, ed. by Joseph N. Moody and Justus George Lawler (Herder and Herder, 1963); *Peace on Earth*, Peter Riga (Herder and Herder, 1964); and *The Social Doctrine of the Catholic Church*, Archbishop Emile Guerry (Alba House, 1961).

The pamphlet and periodical literature on Catholic social teaching is immense. The bound volumes of *Social Order*, *Catholic Mind*, *Review of Social Economy*, *Review of Politics*, *American Catholic Sociological Review*, *America*, and *Commonweal* are rich reservoirs of material. Helpful also are the bound volumes of *Sign*, *Ave Maria*, and the *Catholic World*. For pamphlets, see especially the catalogues of the Paulist Press, America Press, and N.C.W.C.

Two encyclopedias now in preparation, to be published by McGraw-Hill, the *Catholic Encyclopedia* and the *Catholic Youth Encyclopedia*, will have many articles on socioeconomic subjects.

The following books are quoted or referred to in the text:
Effects of Taxation: Investment by Individuals, J. Keith Butters, Lawrence E. Thompson, Lynn L. Bollinger (Cambridge, Mass.: Harvard University Press, 1953);

Characteristics of Stock Ownership, Jean Crockett and Irwin Friend (Ford Foundation Report, 1963);

The Concept of Ethics in the History of Economics, Joseph F. Flubacher (New York: Vantage Press, 1950).

The Affluent Society, John Kenneth Galbraith (Boston. Houghton Mifflin, 1958);

The Other America: Poverty in the United States, Michael Harrington (New York, Macmillan, 1962);

Farms and Farmers in an Urban Age, Edward Higbee (New York: Twentieth Century Fund, 1963);

Laissez-Faire and Communism, John Maynard Keynes (New York: New Republic, 1926);

Essays in Persuasion, John Maynard Keynes (New York: Harcourt, Brace, 1933);

The Share of Top Wealth-Holders in National Wealth, 1922–1956, Robert J. Lampman (Princeton, N. J.: Princeton University Press, 1962);

The Low Income Population and Economic Growth, Robert J. Lampman (Joint Congressional Committee on the Economic Report, 1959);

Principles of Economics, 8 ed., Alfred Marshall (London: Macmillan, 1936);

Taxes for the Schools, Roger A. Freeman (Washington, D.C.: Institute for Social Science Research, 1960);

A Better Economic Order, John A. Ryan (New York: Harper, 1935);

Religion and the Rise of Capitalism, R. H. Tawney (London: Pelican Books, 1938).

The Modern Corporation and Private Property, Adolf A. Berle, Jr. and Gardiner, C. Means (New York: Macmillan, 1932).

Index

Adkins v. Children's Hospital, 43
Advertising, motives stressed in, 185 f
Agency shop, defined, 112
Agriculture, farming as a way of life,
130; flight from the land, 131;
government responsibilities toward,
132; John XXIII on, 131 ff; key
to progress of underdeveloped countries, 158 f; Pius XII on capitalistic
techniques, 130; productivity, 135 f
Aid for International Development,
contribution of, to foreign aid, 153
American Federation of Labor-Congress of Industrial Organization, attitude of Church toward, 96; ethical
codes of, 102; principles of, 95 f
American Motors, profit-sharing plan
of, 125
Antitrust laws, labor unions and, 93
Aquinas, on private property, 27
Arbitration, opposition to compulsory,
105 f; spread of, 103
Aristotle, on private property, 26 f
Automation, and unemployment, 176
Autonomy, of private societies, 89 f

Bentham, Jeremy, a founder of eco-
nomic liberalism, 15 f
Berle, A. A., on corporate power and
its control, 21 f
Big business, John XXIII on, 181
Bigness in business, see Sherman Anti-
Trust Act
Bollinger, Lynn L., on taxes and in-
vestment, 85
Budget, city worker's, 57 ff; cost of, in
selected cities, 59 f
Bureaucrat, vocation of, 184
Butters, J. Keith, on high taxes and
investment, 85

Capitalism, changes in, 21 f; Pius XII
on, 167 ff; reaction to, in Latin America, 167; in the social encyclicals,
169; and stock ownership, 33; in
the U. S., 171 f; see also Economic
liberalism
Catholic Church, see Church
Catholic Interracial Movement, 38
Catholic Relief Services, contribution
of, to foreign aid, 153
Catholic Rural Life Conference, opposition to price support program,

139 ff; program of, 141 ff; supports
family farm, 144 f
Catholic social doctrine, evolution of,
108
Church, attitude toward wealth, 12 f;
reasons for concern about economic
life, 3 f; role in economic life limited, 4 f; social doctrine of, 6 f;
social doctrine not sectarian, 9
Class struggle, Leo XIII on, 99 f;
origin of, 90 f
Clayton Act, on labor as a commodity,
42 f; and labor unions, 93
Closed shop, defined, 111
Collective bargaining, adjustment to
technological progress, 124; effect of,
on working conditions, 103; government intervention in, 121 ff; limitations of, 97 f; see also Labor unions
Colonialism, and foreign aid, 154
Common good, defined, 9; to be respected by private societies, 90
Communism, appeal to underdeveloped
countries, 187; primitive, in early
Church, 26; see also Marxism
Competition, change in nature of, 179;
changes in, 22; concept of fair, 180;
consequences of, 21; Leo XIII on,
17 f; limitations of, 79; Pius XI on,
18; as regulator of collective bargaining, 123; suicidal tendency of,
177; see also Oligopoly; Oligopsony
Cooperatives, commended by John
XXIII, 145; place of, in U. S. farming, 145
Corporations, A. A. Berle and Gardiner
C. Means on, 21 f; growth of, 177 ff;
problem for government, 22
Crockett, Jean, on stock ownership in
U. S., 33

Divine revelation, direct and indirect,
10
Divini Redemptoris, on the family
living wage, 44; on obligation of
social justice, 9

Economic liberalism, attitude toward
labor unions, 90 f; condemned by
Leo XIII, 16 f; John XXIII on, 18 f;
origin of, 14 ff; reaction of Karl
Marx to, 16; theories of, 15 f

191